Building Tax Culture, Compliance and Citizenship

A GLOBAL SOURCE BOOK ON TAXPAYER EDUCATION, SECOND EDITION

OECD
BETTER POLICIES FOR BETTER LIVES

Please cite this publication as:
OECD (2021), *Building Tax Culture, Compliance and Citizenship: A Global Source Book on Taxpayer Education, Second Edition*, OECD Publishing, Paris, *https://doi.org/10.1787/18585eb1-en*.

ISBN 978-92-64-65157-9 (print)
ISBN 978-92-64-72478-5 (pdf)

Photo credits: Cover © designaart-Fotolia.com.

Corrigenda to publications may be found on line at: *www.oecd.org/about/publishing/corrigenda.htm*.

Foreword

This report on taxpayer education builds on the work started in 2013, which led to the publication in 2015 of the report *Building Tax Culture, Compliance and Citizenship: A Global Source Book on Taxpayer Education*. It goes further by not only reviewing the initiatives taking place in 59 developed and developing countries, but also by offering a comprehensive view of the links between those initiatives. It focuses on activities conducted by national tax administrations while acknowledging the importance of civil society regarding taxpayer education.

This report provides internationally comparative data on taxpayer education initiatives and has benefited from input of the members of the OECD Forum on Tax Administration. It aims at being practical by offering a methodology and the necessary knowledge to choose, design and implement new initiatives (or to improve existing ones). We hope it will serve as a guide to development practitioners on how to include taxpayer education modules in their future development co-operation programmes. We also hope that it can be an inspiration for the development of strategies, outreach and literacy campaigns.

Through this report, we aim to further stimulate the global discussion on the importance of taxpayer education, especially in lower-income countries. More broadly, this report is part of the OECD work on tax morale, which seeks to promote research, debate, and action to better understand and encourage voluntary compliance in taxation. It is only through widespread voluntary compliance that countries will be able to raise the revenues necessary to achieve the Sustainable Development Goals.

Acknowledgements

This publication presents the results of two surveys: the first took place in 2019 and focused on taxpayer education initiatives in general; the second took place in late 2020 and sought to understand the effects of the Covid-19 pandemic on those initiatives. It would not have been possible without the direct support and help of many people, particularly the staff in the 59 tax administrations that provided data and country examples, reviewed content, and responded to feedback and questions on the data and text that form the basis of the publication.

The report was prepared by Joseph Stead, Julien Lesavre, Oliver Petzold and Samia Abdelghani, all Advisors in the OECD's Centre for Tax Policy and Administration (CTPA), under the supervision of Ben Dickinson, Head of the Global Relations and Development division of the CTPA. The authors are thankful to Giuliano Festa for his assistance in managing and analysing the initial survey data used to prepare the report, as well as for the work of Daisy Lanvers, Rochana Chalhoub and Zipporah Gakuu for their assistance in preparing the publication. The authors are also thankful to Adriana Ruiz Esparza and Karena Garnier for their assistance in the production of the publication.

The authors are grateful for the feedback provided on early drafts of this report by Professor Marjorie Kornhauser, John E. Koerner Professor of Law Emerita at Tulane University.

Table of contents

FIGURES

TABLES

Reader's guide

Tax Administrations covered by the report

This second edition of *Building Tax Culture, Compliance and Citizenship*, the OECD Centre for Tax Policy and Administration's sourcebook on taxpayer education initiatives, follows that published in 2015 (OECD/FIIAPP, 2015[1]). The primary purpose of this report is to share information that will facilitate dialogue among tax officials, policy makers, researchers and citizens on taxpayer education, tax morale and tax compliance and to help those interested in designing or improving taxpayer education initiatives to do so in the most informed way.

This edition of the sourcebook provides international data from 59 advanced and emerging economies, members and non-members of the OECD.

Data gathering process and reporting

The publication presents the results of an international survey which took place in 2019. Tax administrations were asked to select a limited number (up to three) of what they considered their major taxpayer education initiatives. Survey information was gathered using a form specifically designed for that purpose. Participation was voluntary and 59 tax administrations completed the survey.

While all data contained in the publication has been subject to a high-level review by the OECD, neither the OECD nor any other partner organisation has formally validated the data. As a result, all data included in the publication should be considered as self-reported by the tax administrations concerned.

This initial survey was complemented by a follow-up survey, which focused on the way the Covid-19 pandemic has affected taxpayer education initiatives. Finally, in Spring 2021 the draft report was circulated for comments among all participating countries, as well as members of the OECD Forum on Tax Administration; comments were received from countries which did or did not reply to the first survey and taken into account as extensively as possible. It should be noted that:

- The report aims to show the diversity of taxpayer education initiatives around the world and, through classifying these diverse initiatives into a typology, to help the reader develop a clear picture of existing possibilities and challenges in taxpayer education. The report does not intend to act as catalogue of all the initiatives of participating countries, but rather uses a balanced selection of initiatives to illustrate the various approaches taken. As such, not all initiatives for which information was received are mentioned in the core of the report, though the Annex does contain a summary of all the survey responses.
- Comments received, aimed at clarifying or completing an answer received in the initial survey, were taken into account in the core of the report and/or in the Annex.
- Comments received about initiatives not detailed in the initial survey were mentioned in the text of the report, when appropriate.

- Examples received from countries which did not participate to the initial survey were included in the text of the report, when appropriate.

The publication: structure and use

The main body of the publication is structured around seven chapters:

- the first two chapters comprise an introduction to taxpayer education and the typology created for this report
- this is followed by thematic chapters on teaching tax; communicating tax; providing practical assistance; and the role of non-governmental organisations (NGOs)
- the final chapter offers a conclusion.

This publication is intended to help practitioners, regardless of previous experience, design efficient taxpayer education initiatives adapted to the context of their particular country; to this end, readers may differ in their approach to using this report. The report is designed to provide those wishing to explore the diversity of taxpayer education with an introduction to taxpayer education and a typology, created by this report, as well as more in-depth analysis of the specific issues involved in the different types of initiatives. Readers with precise needs may choose to use the report more selectively; for example those looking for inspiration or guidance on addressing specific challenges may wish to focus on the methodology introduced in chapter one to identify the relevant thematic chapter(s) and initiatives in the Annex.

The publication also contains an Annex that summarises all the initiatives for which tax administrations gave details during the initial survey round, which can be a great resource for all readers.

Abbreviations and acronyms

AFIP	Argentinian revenue authority
ATAF	African Tax Administration Forum
ATO	Australian Taxation Office
BEPS	Base erosion and profit shifting
BSU	Business support unit
CRA	Canadian Revenue Agency
CRNs	Child rights networks
CSC	Civil Society Consortium
CSO	Civil society organisations
CVITP	Community Volunteer Income Tax Programme
DGI	Directorate general for taxes
DGI	Uruguayan tax administration
DGID	General Directorate of Taxes and Government Property (Senegal)
DGT	Directorate General of Taxes (Indonesia)
DIAN	Colombian tax and customs administration
DNI	Directorate National for taxes (Guinea)
ENSEA	École Nationale d'Économie et de Statistiques Appliquées
e-TINs	Electronic tax identification numbers
EY-YTPY	EY Young Tax Professional of the Year
FAQ	Frequently asked questions

FARS	Financial Administration of the Republic of Slovenia
FESPACO	Pan-African Festival of Cinema and Television of Ouagadougou
FIIAP	International and Ibero-American Foundation for Administration and Public Policies
FIRS	Federal Inland Revenue Service (Nigeria)
FPSF	Federal Public Service Finance (Belgium)
FTA	Forum on Tax Administration
FTE	Full-time equivalent
GRS	Georgia Revenue Service
GST	Goods and services tax
HMRC	Her Majesty's Revenue and Customs
HST	Harmonised sales tax
IAPR	Independent Authority for Public Revenue (Greece)
IBP	International Budget Partnership
ICTD	International Centre for Tax and Development
iNOA	Instantaneous Notice of Assessment
IRAS	Inland Revenue Authority (Singapore)
IRD	Inland Revenue Department (New Zealand)
IRS	Internal Revenue Service (United States)
ITA	Israel Tax Authority
KICD	Kenya Institute of Curriculum Development
LB&I	Large Business and International
LO	Liaison officer
MIE	Mauritius Institute of Education
MNE	Multinational enterprise
MTUs	Mobile tax units
NAF	Núcleos de Apoyo Contable y Fiscal

NAFA	National Agency for Fiscal Administration (Romania)
NBR	National Board of Revenues (Bangladesh)
NGO	Non-governmental organisation
NRA	National Revenue Authority (Sierra Leone)
NTA	Norwegian Tax Administration
NTA	National Tax Agency (Japan)
NTS	National Tax Service (Korea)
ODI	Overseas Development Institute
OSIWA	Open Society Initiative West Africa
OTR	Office Togolese des Recettes
PAYE	Pay as you earn
PIT	Private income tax
ROS	Revenue Online Service
RRA	Rwanda Revenue Authority
SARS	South African Revenue Service
SAT	Superintendencia de Administración Tributaria
SII	Servicio de Impuestos Internos
SMEs	Small and medium-sized enterprises
STA	Swedish Tax Agency
STAP	Special Taxpayer Assistance Program (Jamaica)
STI	Lithuanian tax administration
SUNAT	Superintendencia Nacional de Aduanas y de Administración Tributaria (Peruvian tax and customs administration)
TAJ	Tax Administration Jamaica
TAS	OECD Tax Administration Series
TAXEDU	Tax Education Portal (European Commission)
TCA	Tax and Customs Authority (Portugal)

TCE	Tax Counselling for the Elderly
TIN	Taxpayer identification number
TIWB	Tax Inspectors Without Borders
TRA	Tanzania Revenue Authority
TSI	Spanish Tax Studies Institute
UK	United Kingdom
UNDP	United Nations Development Programme
VAT	Value Added Tax
VITA	Voluntary Income Tax Assistance
YEA	Young Entrepreneurs Association

Executive summary

Building tax culture, compliance and citizenship remains as important now as when the OECD published a first report on the topic in 2015. While there has been significant progress in international tax co-operation to tackle fraud, tax avoidance, and tax evasion, important challenges remain in domestic revenue mobilisation. The Covid-19 pandemic has increased demands on states to provide public goods, while reducing economic activity. In this context, mobilising resources requires ambitious fiscal policies backed by robust implementation. Tax administrations' resources, however, are scarce in both financial and human terms. Audits, penalties and other coercive measures have a role to play, but voluntary compliance lies at the heart of all tax systems and so building a taxpaying culture is vital to the domestic revenue mobilisation efforts of countries.

Supporting the efforts of developing countries in taxpayer education is especially important, given the lower levels of taxpayers-per-capita, revenues and tax morale. Developing countries face a combination of challenges: narrow tax bases (resulting in fewer taxpayers), low revenues and low reported levels of tax morale. Therefore, while taxpayer education initiatives are important in all countries, they are especially important to developing countries. They serve as a tool to help reach, and encourage, new taxpayers; explain the role of tax in society; build tax morale; and ultimately increase revenues. It is therefore primarily with developing countries in mind that this report has been prepared, though it is hoped that it will be of use to an even wider audience.

This report builds on the work begun in 2015 to support tax administrations, especially in developing countries, in the design and implementation of taxpayer education initiatives. In response to feedback, the scope has expanded to a broader range of countries of all income classifications and in all geographic regions. To that end, this report builds on the experience of 59 countries gathered through a survey to provide a unique catalogue of the range of taxpayer education initiatives being undertaken around the world. It also proposes a simple four-step methodology that can guide the practical design and implementation of taxpayer education initiatives.

Taxpayer education can take many forms, adapting to local needs (and resources). The 140 initiatives covered by this report (see Annex A) show a wide variation in approach: from student essay writing contests to workshops on complying with new technical regulations; from efforts to inspire the taxpayers of the future while still at school, to assistance in filing this year's returns. Taxpayer education is not only about learning in a formal setting; it is also about communication between citizens and tax administrations, including reminding taxpayers of important deadlines, and being transparent and explaining how revenues are used in a way citizens can understand. Taxpayer education also encompasses reaching out to groups of citizens who have limited contact with the tax administration – for example because they are vulnerable, are far from major cities, or lack access to technology. Taxpayer education initiatives use the full range of communication media, physical and virtual. It is clear that there is no one-size-fits-all approach to taxpayer education, with countries operating under differing resource constraints undertaking a range of initiatives to achieve a number of objectives.

There are, however, clear commonalities among this diversity, enabling the creation of a taxonomy of taxpayer education initiatives and the identification of common approaches, challenges and solutions. All taxpayer education initiatives appear to focus on one of three key approaches:

1. teaching – providing in-depth engagement with the audience which is often, but not always the youth
2. communicating – higher-level engagement focussed on awareness-raising campaigns
3. providing practical assistance – supporting taxpayers directly in their compliance obligations.

This report goes into detail on each of these approaches, identifying common challenges and solutions. It is intended to serve as a valuable resource to inspire and support those designing and implementing taxpayer education initiatives.

Tax administrations are not alone in their focus on taxpayer education. Many of the initiatives featured in this report are conducted in partnership either with other government departments, including local government, or other institutions such as schools, business associations, and non-governmental organisations. Partnerships offer opportunities for expansion and scale that otherwise might not be possible, especially where resources are constrained within tax administrations. In addition, partnerships can help bring access to the target populations, to specific skills and resources, and to logistical support. A number of non-governmental actors also engage in taxpayer education activities independently from the tax administration; while such activities were not part of the survey, their role is analysed in recognition of the important role they can play in taxpayer education.

While there is some positive evidence on the impact of taxpayer education, further efforts are needed to better monitor and evaluate taxpayer education initiatives, especially over the long-term. The survey respondents reported that taxpayer education initiatives had a positive impact in several areas, most clearly on tax morale. However, only half of the initiatives covered in the report were subject to any form of evaluation, highlighting the need to improve the evidence base for the impact of taxpayer education. Even where evaluations had taken place these tended to focus on short-term impacts, despite many having long-term objectives. While evaluation, especially of long-term impacts, may be challenging, it is vital to increasing the understanding of how taxpayer education works, and of how to improve its impact.

The potential of taxpayer education has not yet been realised by all administrations; achieving this will require broader dialogue and deeper integration of taxpayer education into the tax system. All, bar one, of the initiatives covered in the 2015 report are still running, most of them having expanded; there is considerable scope for further expansion, as highlighted by many of the new initiatives covered in this report. The potential to use taxpayer education initiatives to facilitate feedback on tax policy and compliance measures is clear in some countries but is far from universal. Resources are a challenge in many countries and in some there are concerns that taxpayer education may be insufficiently prioritised.

The OECD will continue to encourage the research and development of taxpayer education, and of tax morale more broadly. This report is part of a broader workstream at the OECD, which undertakes new research and encourages global discussions on various aspects of tax morale in developing countries. Covering both businesses and individuals, this workstream recognises the importance of finding tools and approaches to build the intrinsic willingness to pay tax, which is vital for long-term sustainable revenues.

References

OECD/FIIAPP (2015), *Building Tax Culture, Compliance and Citizenship: A Global Source Book on Taxpayer Education*, OECD Publishing, Paris, https://dx.doi.org/10.1787/9789264205154-en. [1]

1 The need for taxpayer education

This chapter introduces the concept of taxpayer education and shows how it can help raise tax morale, compliance and citizenship. It also presents the thematic approach followed in this sourcebook, built around categories and sub-categories of initiatives.

The 2015 report, *Building Tax Culture, Compliance and Citizenship* (OECD/FIIAPP, 2015[1]) **noted that the global recession was slowing down developing countries' efforts to mobilise tax revenues in a sustainable manner** and proposed tools to implement taxpayer education initiatives at a lower cost. Since then, many steps have been taken. A few months after the publication of the 2015 report, the Addis Ababa Action Agenda (United Nations, 2015[2]) was published, followed by the adoption of 17 Sustainable Development Goals (SDG) by the General Assembly of the United Nations, which highlighted the importance of mobilising tax revenues to support all other goals (United Nations, 2015[3]). During the same period, the base erosion and profit shifting (BEPS) package (OECD, 2016[4]), was released comprising 15 reports on reforming the international tax system and tackling tax avoidance. This was followed, in July 2016, by the launch of the Inclusive Framework on Base Erosion and Profit Shifting (OECD, 2016[5]).

The world is undergoing rapid political, economic and social changes, which are reflected in the transformations of the global tax order, in which most countries are working together on an equal footing to improve the international tax system and adapt it to the new realities they face. Co-operation among them has never been deeper, with automatic exchange of information, country-by-country reporting, emphasis on mutual agreement procedures, as well as less visible initiatives, such as Tax Inspectors Without Borders (TIWB), which allows senior auditors from one country to help another country develop skills in a spirit of learning-by-doing (OECD/UNDP, 2019[6]).

All these initiatives aim at tackling tax avoidance and building stronger tax administrations. Mobilising tax revenues remains essential in the current context, where official development assistance is no longer increasing and will not suffice to meet the international commitments (OECD, 2021[7]). As shown by the large number of countries joining the inclusive framework to improve the international tax system, securing or increasing tax revenues is essential to all countries.

Engaging with taxpayers around a culture of compliance is a shared goal between developed and developing countries. Taxpayer education programmes have never been so numerous and diverse, some spreading from country to country and others existing for many years. They enable taxpayers and tax administrations to act as allies in the fight against tax avoidance, corruption and fraud.

Educating taxpayers is a long-term undertaking to which tax administrations are resolutely committed. All but one of the initiatives presented in the 2015 report are still ongoing. The Nigerian "Binding Duty" soap opera reached its natural end before being replaced by many other initiatives, including a new TV broadcast about taxes.

The Covid-19 pandemic is unlikely to change this trend, although it may lead tax administrations to adapt, as priorities change. The pandemic has further increased the need for countries to mobilise resources, as they now need to fund ambitious health and economic recovery plans. The pandemic has also accelerated the movement toward e-administration and the improvement of the online experience of taxpayers.

1.1. What is taxpayer education?

A large number of countries have implemented taxpayer education initiatives in the past few years. The 2015 report (OECD/FIIAPP, 2015[1]) highlighted initiatives from 28 countries from all around the world to help tax administrations choose and implement the most appropriate ones in their countries. The present report is based on survey input from 59 developing and developed countries.

This new report goes further than our previous one and encompasses an even wider range of initiatives in both developed and developing countries. In our previous report, we highlighted the large number of activities and actors involved in taxpayer education programmes. The responses to our survey confirmed the wide variety of initiatives still being implemented around the world. While the previous report focused on the efforts undertaken by national tax administrations in developing countries to show citizens why and how to pay their taxes, the current one includes those of developed countries as well. This results in a more comprehensive study of taxpayer education initiatives.

Taxpayer education is intimately linked to local economic, social and cultural realities. There is no one definition that can fit all country practices and be applicable to all groups of taxpayers. The survey responses made it clear that what is common to all initiatives is their purpose: to transform the relationship among taxpayers, tax systems and tax administrations and to mutually benefit them and society as a whole.

Thus, in this report, taxpayer education includes initiatives aimed at building a culture of tax compliance by:

- **teaching taxpayers**, providing in-depth tuition, building new knowledge and skills;
- using **communication tools to raise awareness in taxpayers** of the different aspects of tax, including obligations, deadlines, taxpayer rights and how taxes are spent; and
- providing taxpayers with **practical assistance** in tax compliance.

This list is not necessarily exhaustive and is not the only possible way to categorise taxpayer education initiatives. Nonetheless, by providing a framework that accounts for the range of initiatives identified, it provides a practical and concrete tool for policymakers and tax administrations wishing to launch or improve taxpayer education programmes.

1.2. How can taxpayer education help?

The mobilisation of domestic resources through taxation is essential to achieve the sustainable development goals as defined in the Addis Agenda, adopted on 16 July 2015. This implies building strong tax administrations and efficient tax systems, as well as tackling tax evasion; but it also calls for creating or strengthening a culture of compliance where the payment of a fair share of taxes is essential to social life and citizenship.

One of the most important changes in the recent past is the way tax administrations view their relationship with taxpayers, moving from coercion to partnership. Increasingly, taxpayers are seen as allies. Threats of penalties for not fulfilling their duties are increasingly being supplemented by the demonstration that by changing their behaviour, they can improve the society in which they live, contribute to its development and free it from external funding.

Paying taxes is a civic duty and taxpayer education is a means to empower taxpayers and to improve tax morale. Several studies have shown that improved tax morale increases tax compliance in a given country (Clifford and Jairus, 2013[8]; Richardson, 2006[9]). Each initiative is unique and is deployed within the specific context of a particular country at a specific moment. It is important to consider the complex characteristics of this context when designing a specific action. For instance, Ritsema et al. (2003[10]) showed that responses to a given initiative vary between groups of taxpayers within the same country.

Tax audits, as opposed to taxpayer education, may not be sufficient to tackle the informal economy, as targeting many taxpayers who owe only a negligible amount of tax requires a significant amount of resources. This is of paramount importance in countries where a significant part of the economy is informal, characterised by the existence of many actors outside established structures, many of whom generate only low incomes. It can be much more effective to mobilise these actors and their clients by strengthening their sense of responsibility and belonging to the community to improve their tax compliance.

In the current research (Mascagni and Santoro, 2018[11]), **taxpayer education is often presented together with deterrence and tax morale as the three components of tax compliance:**

- **Tax deterrence** is linked to penalties and other risks for those who do not comply with their obligations.
- **Tax morale** is generally defined as "the intrinsic motivation to pay taxes" (OECD, 2019[12]), or as "capturing nonpecuniary motivations for tax compliance as well as factors that fall outside the standard, expected utility framework" (Luttmer and Singhal, 2014[13]).
- **Taxpayer education** is often seen as a sharing of knowledge regarding the tax system with taxpayers.

Some research emphasises that taxpayer education can reduce taxpayer lack of knowledge, which has been identified as barrier to compliance. Lack of knowledge is one of the major challenges faced by many tax administrations, but simply telling taxpayers they have to pay taxes is not enough (Moore, 2019[14]). Administrations should try to bridge the knowledge gap through taxpayer education in order to convey to taxpayers the capacity (Ligomeka, 2019[15]) and habit (Mascagni, Santoro and Mukama, 2019[16]) of fulfilling their obligations. However, taxpayers' willingness to pay may not be sufficient. A study by Aiko and Logan (2014[17]) showed that among 62% of the African citizens surveyed, it was difficult to know what taxes they owed. It is thus of major importance to spread tax knowledge across the society, thereby enabling taxpayers to understand how to pay taxes and helping them in doing so.

1.3. The relation between taxpayer education, morale and compliance

One way to grasp this complexity is to further explore the relation between taxpayer education, tax morale and tax compliance. The work of Erzo Luttmer and Monica Singhal (2014[13]) is especially interesting in this regard. They identify five categories of mechanisms that contribute to improving tax morale. The first is "intrinsic motivation", which may be associated with pride, or a good self-image linked to honesty or participation in the public good. The second is "reciprocity", which includes "public goods provided by the state or perceptions of the fairness of the tax system". The third is "peer effect and social influences", which depends on how tax payment is valued in society and how others act towards it. "Long-run cultural factors" is the fourth category of mechanisms they identified and "information imperfections and deviations from utility maximisation" the fifth. The latter mechanism is related to the fact that taxpayers with inaccurate or too little information about the tax system may not comply with obligations they do not understand or may make irrational decisions.

Different forms of taxpayer education may affect different aspects of the relation. For example, taxpayer days or festivals affect three mechanisms (intrinsic motivation, peer effect and long-run cultural factors) while programs designed to help a specific category of the population meet its tax obligations, such as the Special Taxpayer Assistance Program (STAP) in Jamaica, focus more on the latter mechanism, namely "reducing information imperfections".

The countries surveyed were asked to provide an estimate of the impact of each initiative on tax morale: 83% of initiatives were considered to generate a very large or a great increase in tax morale (see Figure 1.1). However, the effects of taxpayer education on tax compliance seem to be more indirect than direct, increasing tax morale, which in turns increases tax compliance.

Figure 1.1. Impact of taxpayer education initiatives on tax morale

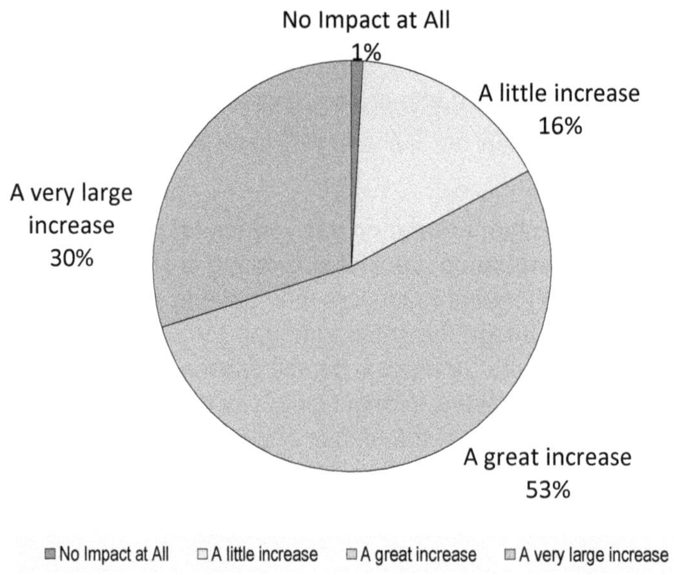

Note: Answers were received for 104 of the 140 initiatives.
Source: OECD Survey on Taxpayer Education Initiatives.

StatLink https://stat.link/e9u0rd

While there is no single definition of taxpayer education, it is a means of empowering taxpayers, giving them knowledge and tools to be able to better understand the tax system, increase their tax morale and finally, increase tax compliance. Nevertheless, it is not a magical tool; initiatives need to be carefully designed to achieve these goals. Despite being cost effective (Mascagni, Santoro and Mukama, 2019[16]), taxpayer education programmes are not free and tax administrations need to invest resources, which may be scarce, especially in developing economies. It is important to understand what kind of initiative will produce the desired result. In that spirit, a few recent studies aimed to measure the effectiveness of specific projects (Casey and Castro, 2015[18]; Mascagni, Nell and Monkam, 2017[19]; Mascagni, Santoro and Mukama, 2019[16]). The present report is part of this trend and aims to provide policymakers, tax administrations and scholars with an overview of existing initiatives and the means to implement them.

1.4. The benefits of taxpayer education

Taxpayer education benefits taxpayers themselves at the scale of the society. The more taxpayers pay their fair share of taxes, the more resources are available to develop the country, build infrastructure and offer services to them. These resources improve taxpayer's daily life and that of their children. The question for taxpayers is no longer, whether they have to pay taxes or not, but rather what they pay taxes for. In a democratic system, taxpayer education can also encourage citizens to support and elect officials who will implement tax policies that will benefit the country.

Moreover, taxpayer education also benefits taxpayers more directly. Tax literacy can help people save money. They may learn, for example, about tax provisions that will legitimately lower their tax bills, or how to avoid filing late or other pitfalls that might cause them to incur fines or penalties. Knowing these benefits exist provides people with an incentive to engage in taxpayer education. It can also increase tax compliance in the long term by increasing tax morale, because tax literacy decreases the time people spend preparing taxes and makes them less threatening. The more taxpayers know about the tax system and the crucial role taxes play in their daily life, the more they can support it.

Tax administrations also benefit from taxpayer education initiatives. It is much easier for them to deal with educated taxpayers because they make fewer mistakes. This allows administrations to redirect their resources to help others or to tackle tax evasion and avoidance.

Educated taxpayers are also better citizens. They not only pay their correct share of taxes on time but they also tend to participate more actively in local debates about taxation. Each educated taxpayer can in turn pass on his or her knowledge and become an agent for the dissemination of tax knowledge in the country.

Taxpayer education leads to increased tax compliance. Ideally, taxpayer education should begin at an early age and continue into adulthood. The aim is for tax administrations to give citizens the opportunity to understand how the tax system works and benefits society as a whole, thus developing a culture of voluntary compliance. In addition, taxpayers must also be continuously and clearly informed of their rights and obligations, of approaching deadlines and of legislative developments to be able to act accordingly. This can be done through information campaigns and awareness-raising activities of the tax administration, such as television and radio broadcasts, publications on taxation or outreach campaigns. Finally, assisting taxpayers in completing their tax returns and encouraging them to use the online services available to them can make their lives easier, save them time, and thus improve their compliance.

A range of well-designed taxpayer initiatives can be complementary. Tax administrations often use different types of programmes concurrently to give taxpayers the appropriate knowledge and tools to understand taxation, their rights, their obligations, and how to comply with them. While many of them use a mix of the three approaches – teaching, raising awareness and assisting – some appear to focus their resources on one category instead. This may be very effective in focusing attention on a particular sector of the population. Nevertheless, by diversifying taxpayer education approaches, tax administrations can benefit from synergies between them and reach a wider population. The best mix will depend on the specific local priorities.

All countries tend to focus their efforts on educating taxpayers at a young age. Non-OECD countries appear to rely more on information campaigns to communicate about taxes. Creating a positive relationship with taxpayers also seems to be more of a concern for non-OECD countries.

Figure 1.2. A global learning experience

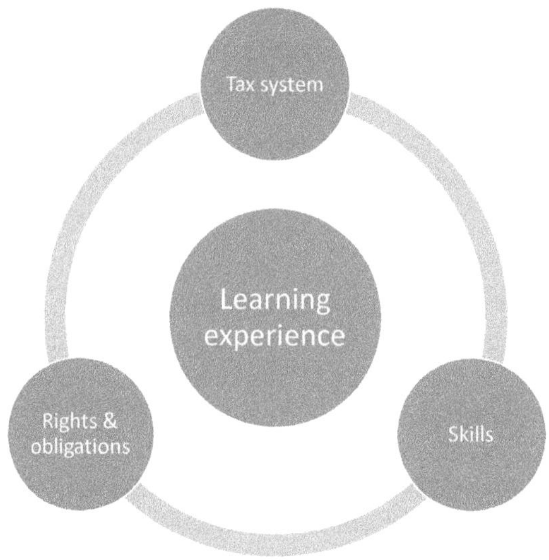

By using different taxpayer education initiatives, tax administrations can offer a comprehensive learning experience on tax, giving taxpayers a better knowledge of their rights and obligations and of the way the system works, as well as helping them develop new skills. In return, taxpayer education may improve the image of tax administrations, give them valuable information to adapt their services, and enhance tax morale and tax compliance. Tax administrations can use this report as a source of inspiration for designing new taxpayer initiatives. To help with this endeavour, the report proposes a step-by-step approach (Box 1.1).

Box 1.1. How to use this report to design taxpayer education initiatives

The present report may be used to foster ideas from all over the world on designing initiatives, identify what kind of initiative is more likely to produce the desired effect and understand the potential challenges faced by implementing it. Prior to designing a taxpayer education initiative, it is important to devote time to defining the objective of the new initiative and the available resources. To assist designers in this task, we propose the following stepwise approach:

Step 1 – Defining a clear objective

The first step is to set the objective in a clear way, as this will help to understand the type of initiative required, narrowing the possible options.

Key questions to help with this process include:

- What is the problem/issue the initiative is expected to address?
- What are the already existing initiatives?
- What kind of information should be communicated to taxpayers and how complex should it be?
- Who is the target audience?
- What are the available resources?

Once these questions are answered it should be easier to clarify the objective, and hence the type of initiative required.

Step 2 – Checking the available resources

Not all initiatives need the same kind of resources. Some are heavily reliant on human resources (tax officials, teachers, etc.) while others may need important funding (to organise a large event). It is essential to have a clear picture of the available resources, as this will be an important element in the choice of the appropriate initiative.

Step 3 – Identifying potential initiatives

The classification provided in this report can offer a guide to identifying the type, or types, of taxpayer initiatives required. While it is not possible to provide an exhaustive guide that covers all possible objectives for taxpayer education, the three broad categories – teaching, raising awareness and assisting – can form the starting point to help gather inspiration from the examples featured in this report.

Teaching tax initiatives (Chapter 3) use more traditional teaching techniques, often to provide more complex information, address issues around the principles and functioning of the tax system, and apply different approaches to different audiences. Awareness-raising initiatives (Chapter 4) use communication tools to provide basic information on the tax system, or to change perceptions of tax/tax administration, while assisting initiatives (Chapter 5) focus on more practical aspects of compliance, either new tools, or lending help to specific groups who have been identified as struggling to comply. In many cases, it will also be possible to identify the relevant sub-category, which can provide further inspiration.

Step 4 – Designing the most appropriate initiative

The following questions may help in designing the most appropriate initiative:

- What challenges may implementation raise?
- Is there a way to overcome them that can be used locally?

- Who are the potential partners (if needed)? Are they willing to participate to the initiative?
- Who (what service, which people, etc.) can organise and manage this initiative?

The current report can provide an overview of potential challenges and partners (Chapters 3 to 5), with advice and recommendations for designing initiatives (Conclusion), as well as with a means of identifying which tax administrations are running similar initiatives (Annex A), allowing designers of new initiatives to contact them to gather more practical information.

1.5. Outline of the rest of the report

This volume builds on the 2015 report (OECD/FIIAPP, 2015[1]), **taking a broader view of the whole landscape of taxpayer education to offer a comprehensive overview of what is being done today.** What is presented here is not a catalogue of initiatives but a guide for those interested in designing, implementing or improving taxpayer education initiatives. Drawing on the large number of initiatives reviewed (140 initiatives in total – see Table 1.1 and Annex A), the report also serves as a useful resource for others researching or analysing taxpayer education.

Table 1.1. Distribution of taxpayer education initiatives by category

	TEACHING			COMMUNICATING			ASSISTING	
	Youth	Business	Individuals	Campaigns	Building relationships	Tailored communication	Using tools & services	Offering direct assistance
OECD countries (28)	18	3	3	9	5	4	5	6
Non-OECD countries (31)	25	11	4	17	14	4	9	10
Total (59)	43	14	7	26	19	9	14	14

Note: While the survey features 140 initiatives, some, called Núcleos de Apoyo Contable y Fiscal (NAF, see Chapter 7) involve simultaneously teaching youth and offering direct assistance. They have been included in both categories.
Source: OECD Survey on Taxpayer Education Initiatives.

The large number of countries (59) which participated in the survey, representing all geographic regions and income levels, provides a truly global picture of taxpayer education initiatives, contributing to the richness of this report. In addition, returning to the countries featured in the 2015 report it appears that most had intensified their efforts, demonstrating the continuing and growing importance given to taxpayer education.

Chapter 2 presents the methodology of the survey as well as its main findings. Chapters 3-5 provide a more detailed look at the different types of initiatives, using specifics from the survey to illustrate the main features and key considerations of each type. While non-governmental actors were not surveyed for this report, Chapter 6 provides a brief overview of some of the roles different types of non-governmental actors can play in taxpayer education. Finally, the ways the Covid-19 pandemic affected taxpayer education initiatives will be discussed in the Conclusion together with recommendations on how to design sustainable taxpayer education initiatives.

References

Aiko, R. and C. Logan (2014), "Africa's Willing Taxpayers Thwarted by Opaque Tax Systems, Corruption", http://dx.doi.org/10.1787/888932807322. [17]

Casey, P. and P. Castro (2015), "Electronic Fiscal Devices (EFDs) An Empirical Study of their Impact on Taxpayer Compliance and Administrative Efficiency", *IMF Working Papers*, No. WP/15/73, International Monetary Fund. [18]

Clifford, M. and A. Jairus (2013), "The effect of Taxpayer education on voluntary tax compliance, among SMEs in Mwanza City - Tanzania", *International Journal of Marketing, Financial Services & Management Research*, Vol. 2/8. [8]

Ligomeka, W. (2019), "Assessing the Performance of African Tax Administrations: A Malawian Puzzle", *ICTD African Tax Administration Paper*, No. 14, International Centre for Tax and Development, Brighton. [15]

Luttmer, E. and M. Singhal (2014), "Tax morale", *Journal of Economic Perspectives*, Vol. 28/4, pp. 149-168, http://dx.doi.org/10.1257/jep.28.4.149. [13]

Mascagni, G., C. Nell and N. Monkam (2017), "One Size Does Not Fit All: A Field Experiment on the Drivers of Tax Compliance and Delivery Methods in Rwanda", *ICTD Working Paper*, No. 58, International Centre for Tax and Development, Brighton. [19]

Mascagni, G. and F. Santoro (2018), "What is the Role of Taxpayer Education in Africa?", *ICTD African Tax Administration Paper*, No. 1, International Centre for Tax and Development, Brighton. [11]

Mascagni, G., F. Santoro and D. Mukama (2019), *Teach to Comply? Evidence from a Taxpayer Education Programme in Rwanda*, http://www.ictd.ac/publication. [16]

Moore, M. (2019), "Intelligent Government: How Research Can Help Increase Tax Compliance", *ATAP Working Paper*, No. 9, International Centre for Tax and Development, Brighton. [14]

OECD (2021), *Development Co-operation Profiles*, OECD Publishing, Paris, https://dx.doi.org/10.1787/2dcf1367-en. [7]

OECD (2019), *Tax Morale: What Drives People and Businesses to Pay Tax?*, OECD Publishing, Paris, https://dx.doi.org/10.1787/f3d8ea10-en. [12]

OECD (2016), *BEPS Project Explanatory Statement: 2015 Final Reports*, OECD/G20 Base Erosion and Profit Shifting Project, OECD Publishing, Paris, https://dx.doi.org/10.1787/9789264263437-en. [4]

OECD (2016), *First meeting of the new inclusive framework to tackle Base Erosion and Profit Shifting marks a new era in international tax co-operation*, https://www.oecd.org/tax/beps/first-meeting-of-the-new-inclusive-framework-to-tackle-base-erosion-and-profit-shifting-marks-a-new-era-in-international-tax-co-operation.htm (accessed on 12 November 2019). [5]

OECD/FIIAPP (2015), *Building Tax Culture, Compliance and Citizenship: A Global Source Book on Taxpayer Education*, OECD Publishing, Paris, https://dx.doi.org/10.1787/9789264205154-en. [1]

OECD/UNDP (2019), *Tax Inspectors Without Borders Annual Report 2018/19.* [6]

Richardson, G. (2006), "Determinants of tax evasion: A cross-country investigation", *Journal of International Accounting, Auditing and Taxation*, Vol. 15/2, pp. 150-169, http://dx.doi.org/10.1016/j.intaccaudtax.2006.08.005. [9]

Ritsema, C., D. Thomas and G. Ferrier (2003), *Economic and Behavioral determinants of tax compliance: Evidence from the 1997 Arkansas tax penalty amnesty program.* [10]

United Nations (2015), *Addis Ababa Action Agenda of the Third International Conference on Financing for Development*, United Nations, New-York. [2]

United Nations (2015), *Transforming our world: the 2030 Agenda for Sustainable Development*, United Nations, New-York. [3]

2 A classification of taxpayer education initiatives

This chapter provides an overview of the proposed classification of initiatives. It describes the three categories and eight sub-categories, as well as how this categorisation can contribute to the analysis of taxpayer education actions carried out around the world.

The broad range of taxpayer education initiatives makes it difficult to provide meaningful analysis without some form of classification. As already identified in the 2015 study, taxpayer education initiatives can take many forms. While this suggests that taxpayer education initiatives can adapt to address the range of objectives tax administrations may have for such initiatives, it also means there is a need for further classification of initiatives to enable analysis and provide useful insights to help others conceptualise, design and implement their own initiatives.

Through the review of 140 initiatives from 59 countries, it is possible to propose a typology of taxpayer education initiatives. A survey was undertaken to provide a global picture of the range of taxpayer education initiatives. By analysing these initiatives, a typology can be proposed, focusing on the approach the initiatives take: in-depth teaching, awareness-raising communication, or providing practical assistance. Each of these three broad categories can be further subdivided to provide a total of 8 categories of taxpayer education initiatives.

This chapter will provide an overview of the survey and the rationale for the classification proposed. In addition, the chapter will draw on data from the survey to provide further analysis, including the distribution of initiative types among developed and developing countries.

2.1. The survey

To obtain a global overview of the range of taxpayer education initiatives implemented by tax authorities, a survey of 59 countries was undertaken. While the 2015 study focussed primarily on developing countries, the intention for this study was to review the global approach to taxpayer education. As such, a survey was sent not only to all the countries featured in the 2015 study, but also to the 53 members of the Forum on Tax Administration. This gave a total of 77 countries to which the survey was sent, of which 59 provided responses.

Two forms of the survey were used: one for countries that had featured in the 2015 study, and another for new countries. Part of the objective of the survey was to track progress in the initiatives featured in the 2015 survey. As such, the slightly different survey sent to those countries that had featured in the previous report featured additional questions regarding progress on the initiatives reported in the 2015 study. Otherwise, the surveys were identical; all countries were encouraged to provide information on up to three initiatives in total. The survey was also made available in English, French and Spanish.

The responses covered a broad mix of countries, both geographically and by level of development. Figure 2.1 shows the distribution of the responses by continent, while Figure 2.2 shows the distribution by income classification. Thus, while the survey was not universal, the responses are sufficiently diverse to promote confidence that the responses cover the range of approaches being taken, offering a sound basis on which to base the classification described in the following section.

Figure 2.1. Responses by continent

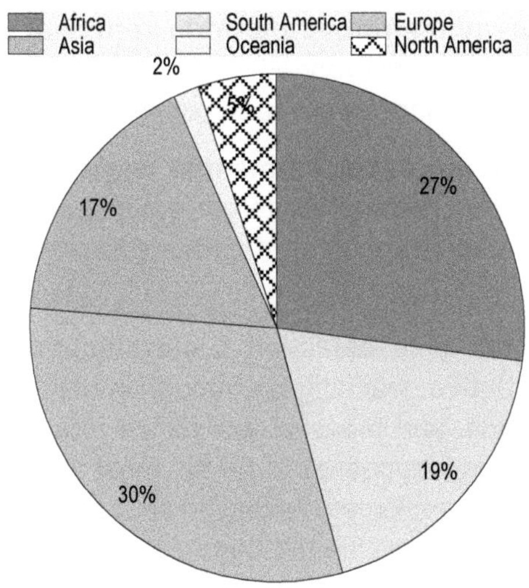

Source: OECD Survey on Taxpayer Education Initiatives.

StatLink https://stat.link/8jgik5

Figure 2.2. Responses by income classification

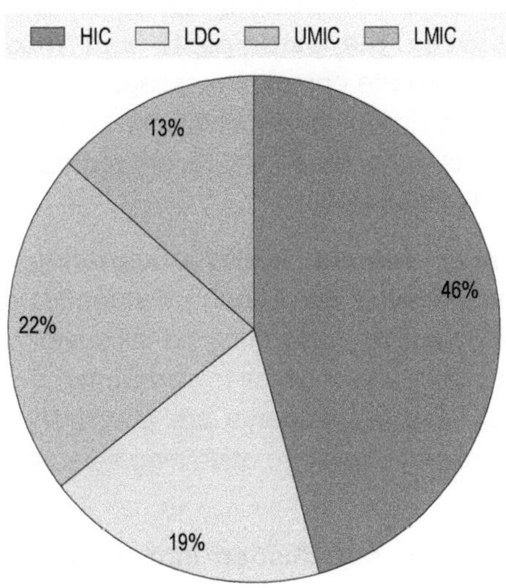

Note: LDC – least-developed country; LMIC – lower middle-income country; UMIC – upper middle-income country; HIC – high-income country.
Source: OECD Survey on Taxpayer Education Initiatives.

StatLink https://stat.link/jl5fkq

2.2. A classification of taxpayer education initiatives

Analysis of the results of the survey reaffirmed the wide variety of taxpayer education initiatives. The initiatives described by tax administrations ranged from essay writing competitions for school children to tax-themed computer games or tax dialogues between businesses and the tax administration.

Such a wide variety means there are several potential ways to approach classifying taxpayer education initiatives. They could be classified by target group (businesses, individuals, children), by delivery mechanism (solely by tax administration or in partnership with others), or intensity of resources required.

The approach taken in this report is to establish a classification that focusses on the broad approach and objective of the initiative: teaching tax through in-depth engagement, communicating tax through awareness-raising campaigns, and practical assistance programmes to directly help taxpayers comply. This approach was chosen as it appeared to be the most practically useful classification for tax administrations looking to design and implement taxpayer education initiatives. The analysis revealed significant similarities across the initiatives within the three categories, especially around the challenges faced and solutions adopted, to provide practical guidance for tax administrations contemplating initiatives of similar types.

It is possible to further break down each of the three main categories to provide eight sub-categories. These sub-categories enable further granularity and make it easier to illustrate the practical approaches undertaken in taxpayer education initiatives (Chapters 3, 4 and 5).

2.2.1. Teaching tax through in-depth engagement

Teaching tax initiatives look to create in-depth engagement with the participants and generally involve interactive dialogue between the participants and those delivering the programme. Teaching tax initiatives seek to communicate complex messages and promote deep thinking among the participants. These messages may vary, from the role of tax in citizenship to more technical aspects of the design and functioning of specific taxes, but they all require an approach that provides the time and space for participants to think, respond and ask questions.

Teaching tax initiatives generally require initial advertising or promotion to encourage participation. In contrast to communicating tax through awareness-raising initiatives, where the first contact with participants is often the objective, in teaching tax initiatives participants often need to be made aware of the initiative first, and then invited to register to participate. While this is not the case where tax is included in the school curriculum, and the students are effectively a captive audience, many of the school-based initiatives identified a related challenge of gaining awareness across the schools/teachers to enable the initiative to be delivered.

Teaching tax initiatives can be further sub-divided into three sub-categories, according to the target audience. The responses from the survey highlighted the varying approaches taken to different audiences, especially regarding the types of partnerships required to successfully deliver the initiatives. Given the intensive nature of these initiatives, partnerships appear important, be they with schools, teachers and ministries of education when teaching students; with business associations when delivering workshops to businesses; or with groups and associations with links to vulnerable groups when seeking to work with individuals.

Of the 140 initiatives reviewed, 64 aim at Teaching Tax (44 %); these were widely distributed globally. The most common (43 initiatives) focussed on students, followed by those focussed on businesses (14) and individuals (7).

2.2.2. Communicating tax through awareness-raising campaigns

Communicating tax initiatives are focussed on raising awareness among taxpayers regarding different aspects of the tax system. This can include awareness of rights and obligations or of changes in the tax system, or may address issues facing specific groups of taxpayers or promote improvements in the perception of the tax system and administration.

Communicating tax initiatives is often effectively a form of advertising, with less scope for dialogue and feedback. While some initiatives, especially those employing behavioural science approaches, can generate valuable data, in general, the communicating tax initiatives are more one-directional (and in some cases relatively passive), disseminating specific messages to the chosen audience. The focus of these initiatives is therefore often on the first impression; unlike Teaching Tax initiatives they do not generally seek deeper participant engagement in the initiative.

Communicating tax initiatives can be further sub-divided into three sub-categories, focussing on the objective of the communication. The responses from the survey identified similarities between initiatives with related objectives. While information campaigns may seek to communicate different information on the tax system, they all face similar challenges in identifying the right audience and selecting the best form through which to communicate the message. Initiatives focussed on building a positive image of the tax administration are united in addressing the challenge of how to present the tax system in a new light. Tailored initiatives all look at ways in which the messaging can be refined to target specific groups, or to nudge behaviour in a specific way.

The survey found that 53 initiatives focus on communicating tax (36%). Information campaigns are the most common (26 initiatives), but an increasing number of countries are aiming to build a stronger and more positive relationship with taxpayers through events or games (19). Both the information campaigns and initiatives looking at building a positive relationship are much more common in non-OECD countries, which provided 17 of the examples of information campaigns and 14 of the positive relationship examples. Tailored messaging to groups of taxpayers had eight examples, equally divided between OECD and non-OECD countries.

2.2.3. Practical assistance initiatives

Practical assistance initiatives provide direct assistance to taxpayers in fulfilling their compliance obligations. Tax can be complex, especially for those unfamiliar with the compliance processes. For this reason, practical initiatives are an important part of taxpayer education in a number of countries.

Practical assistance initiatives can be integrated within the development of new tools and services. While new, generally digital tools and services are designed to make compliance easier, some taxpayers need support to encourage them to move to new tools. Practical assistance programmes can help in such transitions.

Practical assistance initiatives can be split into two sub-categories. The main difference identified in the survey in practical assistance initiatives was that a number of initiatives were specifically linked to the development and deployment of new tools and services; this creates additional considerations in comparison to initiatives that did not have such a link.

Providing practical assistance to taxpayers was the aim of 30 initiatives (20%). Non-OECD countries were more likely to identify this kind of initiative, providing 19 of them.

2.3. Eight sub-categories to cover all taxpayer education initiatives

As outlined above, the three main categories can be subdivided to provide a more complete classification. Figure 2.3 shows the full classification.

Figure 2.3. The taxpayer education classification

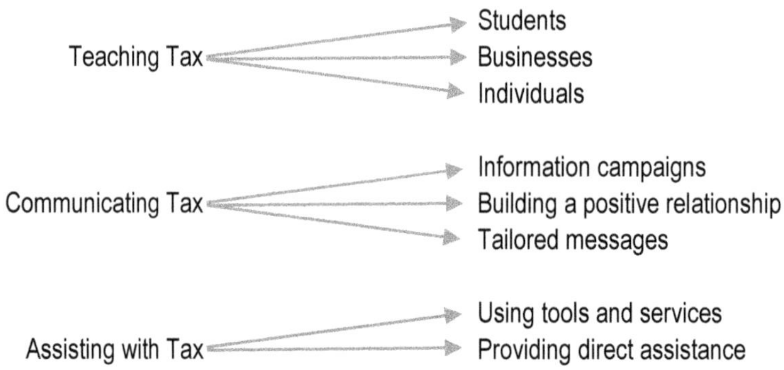

Figure 2.4 shows the distribution of examples provided in the survey across the sub-categories. The most frequently used types of initiatives per category are **teaching youth** (29%) to share knowledge about taxes and tax systems, **information campaigns** (18%) to communicate on tax, and **offering direct assistance** (11%) to make taxpayers' life easier. Nearly one initiative out of two therefore belongs to either the teaching youth or information campaign categories.

Figure 2.4. The eight sub-categories of initiatives

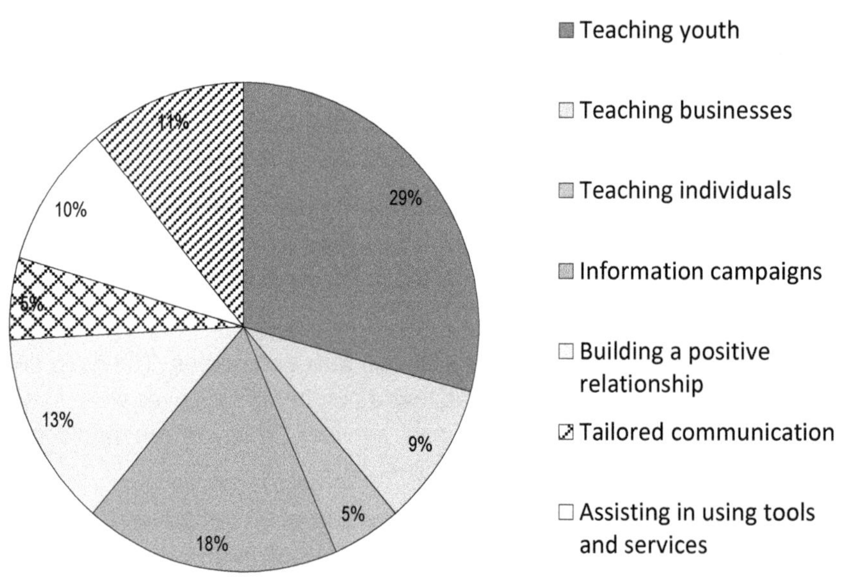

Source: OECD Survey on Taxpayer Education Initiatives

StatLink https://stat.link/7a15nj

2.3.1. Teaching tax to students

The results of our survey clearly show that tax administrations put a great emphasis on educating future taxpayers. Out of the 59 responding countries, 27 had at least one such programme up and running and 12 had more than one. Tax administrations are very creative, and the range of existing programmes is very broad, but one common feature is that they allow for reaching most of the children in a cohort. Some involve classroom teaching or debates, managed by the teacher or a tax official, while others allow students to experience tax administrations themselves. The aim is not to say, "paying your taxes is important", but to show why it is important: because it helps to build a better society.

These initiatives are collaborative in the sense that to be successful, other actors need to be involved. This can include, for example, ministries of education at a global level, or schools or universities at a more local one.

Teaching tax culture and citizenship at school is a long-term project which helps spread a culture of tax compliance in the entire society. This is not easy, as it requires the involvement of a wide range of actors (from teachers to ministries of education, universities and schools, etc.). It implies finding the right way to communicate with them (directly with school principals, through NGOs or ministries of education) without imposing an excessive burden on them. To address the latter point, tax authorities are making efforts to make materials available to teachers, for example on a dedicated page of their website. Teachers are in direct contact with students, and they first need to be convinced of the importance of taxation to then be able to carry an inspiring message to the youth. Thus, tax administrations must include actions directed at teachers in their programmes, or to have tax officials go to schools to directly share their knowledge.

Furthermore, to be effective programmes for youth need to be consistently pursued over years. This is a difficulty shared by all initiatives aiming at educating taxpayers, but it is more acute here because to maximise the effect of the programme it is desirable that students be exposed to education programmes at different levels during their studies, in primary and secondary school as well as at university. Schools and universities are also a good environment for more ludic initiatives like contests and competitions around tax issues. As in Japan, Lithuania or Spain, these can be fun and can make students think for themselves about why it is wrong to evade taxes.

Getting young people to work with tax authorities is an innovative way of using existing civil service programmes to help build a tax compliant society. These programmes are generally seen as a good way to improve citizenship by giving young people a sense of belonging to the nation. Their use as a means of educating future taxpayers is one way to achieve both objectives simultaneously.

In a world of instantaneity, it is interesting to see that tax administrations are thinking long term by favouring programmes with incremental effects over time. These programmes are, nevertheless, rarely used alone and out of the 27 countries having programmes to educate youth, 21 have other on-going programmes.

2.3.2. Education initiatives for businesses

Businesses and especially small and medium-sized enterprises (SMEs) are also priority targets in many countries. In fact, 11 countries reported running programmes to better educate businesses, which can take the form of face-to-face meetings or seminars or use digital tools like webinars to reach a large audience.

Businesses may be concerned by a wide range of taxes and need precise and up-to-date information to be able to cope with their obligations. The level of technical detail to be provided is often high, requiring an approach that offers the time and space to convey all the information required, enable questions to be posed, and allow the content to evolve in response to the needs of the audience. For these reasons, these initiatives often take the form of seminars or meetings about a specific tax issue. Some tax administrations adapt their communication by focusing on specific, high-risks sectors or by asking in advance the issues that given taxpayers wish to see addressed.

Developing programmes for the public may be difficult due to logistical issues (especially when gathering a large number of taxpayers together). Webinars can help but they necessitate taxpayers being well connected to the Internet, and that is not always the case. One way to address this is, instead of having multiple taxpayers come to tax administrations, tax officials can hold the seminar either in the premise of a participating company or in a local municipal facility.

Webinars are often used to broaden the audience and to reduce costs for tax administrations and taxpayers, as they help keep logistics minimal. One additional benefit of webinars is that they can be recorded and replayed later, allowing the creation of a library of webinars covering all major areas of taxation.

2.3.3. Education initiatives for individuals

Individuals may greatly benefit from education programmes. However, the individuals tax administrations face are not standard and programmes have to be tailored to the specific audience they wish to target.

Tax administrations do not always directly manage those programmes. Some are run with the help of civil society organisations acting as a proxy for tax administrations. Instead of directly assisting taxpayers, tax administrations train the members of organisations that are already well established and recognised in the country, which can in turn educate individuals that tax administrations would not have been able to reach otherwise.

Other education programmes indirectly benefit individuals. This includes, for instance, the parents of pupils who explain what they learnt at school about how paying taxes helps to build a fairer society or the person attending seminars about business and taxes. This may be the reason why education initiatives are less often directed toward individuals (6 countries have programmes targeting individuals, 11 targeting businesses and 27 targeting youth).

It is also important for individuals to be aware of the existence of education programmes if they are to engage with them. This issue, shared by all kinds of programmes and by tax administrations in general, is so important that many tax administrations are actively raising awareness about taxes and tax systems.

2.3.4. Information campaigns

Information campaigns are widely used; in fact, they are the second most used means of educating taxpayers; 23 of the 59 surveyed administrations reported using them. It is worth noting that in a few countries (3), information campaigns are the only means of taxpayer education (even if some run several of them).

Information campaigns are a good means of increasing taxpayers' sense of belonging to the community. Tax administrations are accountable to citizens through their representatives in parliaments, but in practice it is important to demonstrate this accountability in a more direct way. This implies demonstrating how taxes are spent to benefit the whole community.

Building a sense of belonging through tax also necessitates taxpayers not only knowing their obligations, but also their rights. Tax administrations can help with this through information campaigns, publications or social media.

Providing taxpayers with basic information may be helpful for some, but in the era of rich content, information campaigns have gone beyond simply informing taxpayers. They put information in context, explain it, simplify it, synthesize it and allow taxpayers to appropriate it. The choice of media used to reach out to taxpayers is essential as different media have characteristics which may be more suitable to one kind of message or another. What makes information campaigns so popular amongst tax administrations is their ability to reach the entire population of a country, or at least most of it, including people living in remote areas. It is particularly suitable for initiatives tackling the informal sector, focusing on customers and on changing their behaviour. Asking for a receipt may seem nothing to most people, but it may make a huge difference nationwide; information campaigns are great to explain how a simple gesture can make societies better.

Covering or targeting the right audience is a first step but designing a message that is understandable and that can change people's minds remains a difficult task. Ensuring that a message is user friendly makes it easier to be shared and accepted. Another way to ensure that messages have a significant impact on a category of taxpayers is to work with them, either gathering information through other taxpayer education initiatives (during events or using more scientific methods) or by exposing a few members of the target audience to the message and gathering their feedback to improve it.

2.3.5. Building a positive relationship

Tax days, fairs and other events are great means of building a more positive relationship with taxpayers. They commonly take place during a limited period, from a day up to a week. They can comprise several activities taking place at different locations throughout the country. Their main strength is that they create a space where taxpayers and tax officials can meet. This can be done around activities for kids or with stands set up for the occasion. This can also give the opportunity to thank taxpayers by awarding the best taxpayers of the year.

Such events, and especially tax days or tax weeks, can be part of a broader political agenda to strengthen citizenship; in this case, high officials from the government may be involved, sending a powerful message to the country. These events are often supported by a strong narratives going beyond taxation, for instance linking paying taxes with freeing the country from foreign aid (Luttmer and Singhal, 2014[11]) or strengthening the country, as in Côte d'Ivoire; or even gathering the country around a common goal, as in Guatemala. Even when this is not the case, however, it is possible to associate celebrities with the event to drastically improve its visibility and to build on the reputation of that person.

However, organising such events can be costly and challenging for tax administrations and some of them prefer to be part of events already organised in the country. These are places where many people already go for other reasons than to get information on taxes, and where it is possible to start a fruitful discussion with them.

Other media can also be used by tax administrations to get in touch with taxpayers in their daily life. Especially in Africa, some tax administrations have institutionalised short regular broadcasts aired just before the evening news. These broadcasts deal with a different subject each time and are generally proposed by an official of the tax administration. They are a good way to promote tax citizenship, inform taxpayers and shed light on the women and men working in tax administrations. They are also a good way to make sure taxpayers are aware of their rights and obligations, as this is the foundation of tax compliance and citizenship.

Another fun way to engage with young people is to take advantage of existing entertainment technologies, such as videos or apps. Many countries use them in an effective way, for instance producing games or music videos.

2.3.6. Tailored communication to specific groups of taxpayers

While mass media are extremely useful for reaching wide audiences, specific groups of taxpayers sometimes need more tailored messages.

Tax administrations are eager to work with researchers and scholars to better understand the needs and behaviours of taxpayers. The relationship is beneficial for both parties, as tax administrations benefit from the knowledge produced and methods of analysis deployed, while in return, researchers benefit from the already identified topics of interest and the large amount of information available to understand them. For instance, tax administrations send letters or emails to taxpayers (individuals or businesses) that have not paid their taxes on time and researchers can help understand what message would be the most efficient to convince them to pay.

Researchers can rely on proven methods to produce reliable results. They can do quantitative statistical research, such as that mentioned above, but they can also do more qualitative analysis based on ethnographic methods. In both cases, the goals remain the same: understanding taxpayers. This new knowledge can be used to offer a better service or to improve communication.

2.3.7. Assisting taxpayers in complying with their obligations

Small businesses and individuals may greatly benefit from the assistance of tax administrations in filing their income tax returns. By doing so, tax administrations do not only assist the individuals receiving the help, but also the whole country as this greatly increases the level of compliance. When tax administrations offer such a service to taxpayers in specific locations, they can do so through their regular offices but also by opening temporary service points. This is of major importance, especially for reaching taxpayers located far from regular offices or facing difficulties in reaching the locations (either because they must run their business or because of a lack of affordable transport). Another efficient way to offer the service to those who need it the most is to use mobile units such as the ones used in South Africa. Those are moving offices that can be deployed where they can be the most useful. For those units to be as efficient as possible, it is important that taxpayers be aware of their temporary location. Having many of them allows for greater visibility and efficiency, but this is an investment that not all tax administrations can make.

As already mentioned above, civil organisations, like business-related associations or others, can be very efficient in reaching taxpayers. Their members need to be appropriately trained to become tax administrations spokespersons. They have the advantage of knowing specific groups of taxpayers and speaking the same "language".

2.3.8. Assistance in the use of tax tools and services

While many tax tools and services can make compliance easier, for some taxpayers assistance may be required to enable them to effectively use such tools and services. The objective of these initiatives is not to undertake specific tasks for or with taxpayers, but to train them to use tools or services specially designed to ease their life. Such tools can be as simple as a pre-filled tax return or as complex as a fully online platform covering the whole range of declarations and services taxpayers may need. Such initiatives may be a complement to other initiatives; while one may communicate the existence of such tools and services, raising awareness, a more practical assistance-focussed initiative can support those who are identified as needing more hands-on help.

E-services are the focus of many initiatives in this category. Many countries have introduced e-services in recent years, and even if the scope of the reforms may differ, they all aim at simplifying the filing process and offering easily accessible services. These projects are ambitious and often integrated within a broader vision of the country.

Providing taxpayers with a single, secure access point is one of the most common tools implemented in recent years. Such access points help simplify the relationship between taxpayers and tax administrations by grouping available services together. This approach also helps in reducing costs for tax administrations (as there tend to be fewer errors) and for taxpayers (as online forms are designed to be easier than paper forms).

Once new tools are developed, it is necessary to advertise them and train taxpayers to use them. This is often the subject of a wide communication plan using all other means of taxpayer education, like information campaigns, direct communication to taxpayers (through events, emailing, phone calls, etc.), the production of leaflets and training programmes.

The assistance takes different forms depending on the tool. For instance, when the new tool is an online pre-filled tax return, an information campaign explaining that most taxpayers can complete their return in a few clicks may prove efficient. However, when the tool is complex or is the first of its kind among the administrations of a country, a more ambitious plan may be needed, for instance with an online video explaining the different steps and options offered by the new tool.

2.4. Evaluations and impacts

Only half (72/140) of the initiatives were subject to any form of evaluation and only 25 (18%) were subject to external evaluation. The limited level of evaluations across the initiatives makes it difficult to draw many conclusions, apart from highlighting the need to invest further in evaluations. For teaching initiatives, 56% were evaluated, which is more than awareness-raising initiatives (47%) or assistance initiatives (40%). External evaluations were not evenly distributed among the categories: no assistance initiative benefited from such evaluation, while 19% of teaching initiatives and 22% of awareness-raising initiatives did.

Where evaluations did take place, many appear to have looked at short-term impacts. Where details of evaluations were provided, these tend to be surveys/questionnaires of the participants assessing the quality of the teaching/communication materials. As a result, there is very limited data from formal evaluations on the long-term impacts of taxpayer education initiatives on taxpayer behaviour. While such assessments are inevitably difficult to undertake, this research gap needs to be addressed.

Respondents were asked to provide their own estimates of the impact of the initiatives in several key areas. Given that most initiatives have not been evaluated, and none appear to have been evaluated on all the aspects covered by the impact's questions, the responses here are clearly only perceptions. Nevertheless, they may provide a useful indication of where taxpayer education programmes are perceived to be having the most impact.

The teaching initiatives were perceived to have the greatest impact on tax morale. Among respondents, 90% perceived teaching tax initiatives to have a great or very large impact on increasing "people's sense of moral obligation to pay taxes 'voluntarily'" (i.e., tax morale), compared to 76% for awareness raising and 75% for tax assistance.

The assistance initiatives were perceived to have the biggest impact on taxpayer knowledge. While all categories of initiatives were perceived as having a great or very large impact on increased taxpayer knowledge (between 78 and 85%), **there is a great discrepancy in the top rating of "very large increase"**; 52% of respondents saw the assistance initiatives as having a very large impact on increased knowledge compared to 27% and 33% for awareness raising and teaching, respectively.

Awareness-raising initiatives were estimated to have the least impact on participants' perceptions that "the government spends their tax money wisely"; 12% responded that awareness-raising initiatives had no impact on the belief that governments spend their tax money wisely; a further 40% estimated only a small impact, for a total of 52% seeing no or little impact. This compares to 44% and 33% of respondents who consider assistance to taxpayers and tax teaching initiatives, respectively, have no or little impact.

Awareness-raising initiatives were also perceived to have the least impact on perceptions that "other taxpayers are paying their fair share": 52% of respondents saw these initiatives as having little or no impact on perceptions that other taxpayers were paying their fair share, compared to 37% for tax teaching initiatives and 21% for taxpayer assistance initiatives. Interestingly, the taxpayer assistance initiatives had the highest share of perceptions with relation to both having a very large impact (21%) and no impact at all (14%).

2.5. Summary

The present report gathers information on 140 initiatives from 59 countries, grouped under three main categories (teaching taxpayers, communicating tax and assisting taxpayers) and eight subcategories. These divisions are designed to help policymakers and tax administration officials easily find initiatives that are relevant to achieving their goals in terms of taxpayer education, as well as practical advice on implementing them. The following chapters will describe each initiative type, with an analysis of objectives, policy options, suggestions from tax administrations concerning implementation, and observed and potential impacts.

Chapter 3 presents initiatives focussed on teaching essential elements of the tax system. Their aim is to strengthen tax culture, build a culture of voluntary compliance, explain the benefits of paying taxes and – in general – increase tax morale. The subcategories of initiatives are divided by target: future taxpayers (i.e., primary, secondary, and university students – sec. 3.1); businesses (both SMEs and big companies – sec. 3.2); and individual taxpayers (with a special focus on activities reaching out to lower middle-income taxpayers, taxpayers living in rural areas, etc. – sec. 3.3).

Chapter 4 is devoted to initiatives to communicate tax, raise awareness and inform people regarding tax and the tax system. The information provided through these initiatives – although still aiming indirectly at raising tax morale and culture – has more narrow and direct objectives. Specific information campaigns (sec. 4.1) can aim at: giving particular information to some segments of taxpayers to increase their knowledge of the tax system and of tax rights and obligations (e.g. explaining tax obligations to new entrepreneurs and foreigners, guides for property owners, information for auditors, etc.); increasing compliance (e.g. organising receipt lotteries to motivate taxpayers to check receipts, publishing documents and distributing them to specific audiences, conducting awareness campaigns, etc.); providing information and updates on the tax system and new tax laws (e.g. via social networks, call centres, and TV and radio programmes). For many tax administrations, however, it is also essential to build a strong and positive relationship with taxpayers (sec. 4.2) through tax events and fairs like National Taxpayer Days as well as through regular TV shows or games. Section 4.3 is dedicated to highlighting the importance of tailored communication for reaching specific groups of taxpayers. Some tax administrations are in the process of improving such communications using scientific methods (like behavioural insights and ethnographic research) to better understand audiences and be more effective.

Chapter 5 discusses assistance initiatives aimed at easing the life of taxpayers, namely through the use of new tools and services (e.g., e-services such as e-filing, web portals, new tax laws, etc. – sec. 5.1) and assistance in filing returns (sec. 5.2). These constitute a more practical type of taxpayer education.

Chapter 6 focuses on non-tax administration actors such as NGOs. Finally, Chapter 7 concludes with the lessons learnt and provides suggestions and recommendations for increasing the success of taxpayer education initiatives.

The Annex A summarises all the initiatives for which tax administrations gave details during the initial survey round.

References

Luttmer, E. and M. Singhal (2014), "Tax morale", *Journal of Economic Perspectives*, Vol. 28/4, pp. 149-168, http://dx.doi.org/10.1257/jep.28.4.149. [1]

3 Teaching tax essentials

This chapter looks at more formal and intensive taxpayer education initiatives, as well as the challenges and solutions to effective design and implementation. While most initiatives are focussed on students undergoing formal education, there are also those aimed at businesses and individual taxpayers.

Tax can be complicated, especially for those with little or no existing knowledge of the tax system. Students, adults, business owners, employees and vulnerable groups may all lack sufficient understanding of the design and working of the tax system, limiting their ability to engage effectively with it. Encouraging citizens to develop an appreciation of and commitment to the role of tax in society and ensuring that taxpayers and employees responsible for tax compliance are aware of their roles and responsibilities, can be a significant challenge.

Providing sufficiently intensive and in-depth taxpayer education to overcome complexity, make people more comfortable with their role in the tax system, and encourage long-term behaviour can therefore be a useful approach. Where the existing knowledge of the tax system is minimal, or understanding of vital detail is lacking, there is a need for an in-depth approach that provides an opportunity for deeper engagement by participants.

This chapter looks at a range of intensive taxpayer education initiatives which seek a more substantial engagement with participants. In contrast to the initiatives covered in Chapter 4, which are focussed on awareness-raising/mass marketing of tax and where the engagement with taxpayers is often short, the commonality among the initiatives covered in this chapter is a longer and/or deeper engagement with the participants, which creates specific challenges and considerations.

These initiatives are often resource-intensive and benefit significantly from partnerships, especially when seeking to expand. A common trait of the initiatives featured in this chapter is they tend to be resource-intensive. Reliance on face-to-face instruction is a key factor behind the resource commitment for many of the initiatives, though webinars are increasingly an alternative and can reduce the resources required. The resource requirements, especially the human resource requirements, often limit the scale of the initiatives unless partnerships can be established to share them.

While in-depth and intensive taxpayer education initiatives can be used in a variety of contexts, they are especially common with students. Encouraging voluntary compliance as early as possible has the greatest potential returns over time, creating an obvious benefit by building a durable understanding of and commitment to the tax system in the taxpayers of the future. The school system also provides an established network through which to deliver such programmes, whereas similar in-depth initiatives for adults face additional hurdles in establishing a delivery network.

More substantive taxpayer education initiatives also facilitate feedback and dialogue, helping identify challenges and possible improvements to the tax system. Especially in initiatives with businesses the added value of being able to obtain feedback from taxpayers on how the tax system is working (or not) was consistently highlighted as a benefit of the more in-depth style of initiatives covered in this chapter.

This chapter looks in detail at in-depth taxpayer education initiatives with different audiences – students, businesses and individuals – identifying common features, challenges and solutions. While there are some broad common features across all the initiatives, there are also specific features depending on the audience. The chapter therefore goes into detail to provide practical lessons for those thinking of implementing similar programmes.

Further details on 64 of the initiatives analysed to inform this chapter can be found in Annex A.

3.1. Taking tax to students

Tax morale generally appears to increase with age, which indicates potential gains in changing behaviour earlier. In the 2019 report *Tax Morale* (OECD, 2019[1]), age was found to be one of the prime determinants of tax morale globally, with older people less likely to justify cheating on taxes. This suggests that significant gains can be made by targeting efforts to promote the need to pay taxes among younger generations. Establishing a taxpaying habit early in a citizen's life can return a significant dividend over the years.

Teaching tax to children can also be part of broader citizenship education. Educating children and teenagers on tax matters offers an opportunity to build the social contract, helping children see the social utility of taxes, from their use to finance public services and institutions such as schools, hospitals and the police to their redistributive function. At its most ambitious, it can help children identify not just their own rights and responsibilities, but also those of the state with regards to transparency and accountability over how taxes are spent. For example, in Guatemala the Tax Culture Training Programme was established in 2007 to teach tax as a fundamental aspect of citizenship among Guatemalans.

Integrating tax education into the education process is one of the most popular taxpayer education methods, though a range of approaches are taken globally. In the survey, initiatives targeting youth were the single most common type of initiative reported, with 43 examples provided by the 59 countries responding to the survey. Box 3.1 shows the reach of several of these programmes. There is clearly no standard approach, however, and the examples provided were varied, including: using modules on tax culture and citizenship in primary and secondary schools; conducting essay contests on tax culture; sending tax officers to schools to give presentations and have debates with students; and temporarily transforming students into civil servants.

Box 3.1. The reach of future taxpayer focussed initiatives in several countries.

- Colombia: 94 schools participating
- Guatemala: 1 750 students face-to-face / 10 000 students virtually per year
- Israel: 250 schools (25% of high schools) / 30 000 students in 2018
- Ivory Coast: 4.7 million students per year
- Italy: over 1 500 meetings with students per year
- Mauritius: 30 000 students per year
- Peru: 45 195 students / 1 263 teachers / 365 schools / 500 active volunteers in 2018
- Romania: over 2 000 students in 2018
- South Africa: 65 000 teachers and students in 2017/18
- Spain: 45 000 students in 2018
- Turkey: 5 million students per year
- Zambia: 25 900 students per year

Source: OECD Survey on Taxpayer Education Initiatives.

3.1.1. Selected policy options

Putting tax on the curriculum

Integrating tax within school curricula has the potential for reaching (nearly) all future taxpayers. Schemes at the primary or secondary school level can aim for universal coverage across entire cohorts. For example, Mauritius introduced tax into the curriculum for grade 7 and 8 students (age 12-13) while Kenya expanded the school outreach programme highlighted in the 2015 report by starting to integrate tax into the curriculum of "carrier subjects", such as History and Social Studies (Box 3.2). Such broad programmes are not simple to implement, however, requiring strong partnerships and significant resources.

Effective collaboration is needed between tax administrations and education ministries for school-based initiatives to grow to scale. Several countries (including Kenya and Mauritius) highlighted collaboration with the ministry of education (or the equivalent institution responsible for regulating curriculum content) as a vital partnership. This is necessary to enable teaching tax in schools to go beyond ad hoc partnerships with individual schools, becoming widespread and embedded as part of the standard curriculum.

Box 3.2. Integrating tax into the Kenyan curriculum

As outlined in the 2015 report, Kenya established a school outreach programme in 2012. It provided for the Taxpayer Education Unit of the Kenya Revenue Authority to attend schools providing lessons and lectures on taxation, as well as training for students. At the time of the 2015 report, over 25 000 students had been reached.

Since the 2015 report, the scheme has continued to be successful and has expanded. The challenges of limited financial and human resources had already been identified at the time of the 2015 report. The Taxpayer Education Unit realised the need to establish a more sustainable long-term strategy to address this problem, mainstreaming tax education into the curriculum. Working with the Kenya Institute of Curriculum Development (KICD), the process is underway to introduce tax into a number of "carrier" subjects, including languages, mathematics, history, religious education and social studies. The roll-out began with grade 4 of the primary schools and will expand to other grades in due course.

The partnership with the KICD has been vital, enabling a scale and reach for the initiative that would have been impossible for the Taxpayer Education Unit to achieve alone.

Source: OECD Survey on Taxpayer Education Initiatives.

Tax administrations need to provide resources to support both students and teachers. While in some cases tax administration staff are responsible for delivering teaching on tax, they usually lack the resources to do so, especially in large-scale programmes where tax is part of the national curriculum. Instead, the role of the tax administration is generally to produce materials tailored to the educational level of the students targeted, often making them available online or through schoolbooks. One aspect highlighted by Argentina (Box 3.3) is the need to provide resources not just for the students, but also for the teachers, explaining the aims of the initiatives and how to use the resources. This is especially important where awareness and understanding of the tax system are generally low, as it may not be possible to assume that teachers are sufficiently tax literate.

Box 3.3. Teaching tax in school in Argentina

The Argentinian revenue authority (AFIP) decided to target building students' understanding of tax and of the role of tax in society. As AFIP wanted to ensure the continuity of the programme, a close alliance with the education system was sought. This approach was challenging, requiring the establishment of inter-institutional teams, regular meetings with the key actors in the education system, and agreements and collaboration with provincial governments. It also required significant investment in the creation of materials, and crucially the training of teachers to enable them to become agents of change and make tax integral to their teaching of citizenship.

The programme is viewed as successful, with an external evaluation from the University of Buenos Aries identifying high satisfaction and knowledge retention among participants. The investment in building support among multiple institutions also provided some resilience for the programme in the face of changes in management priorities, as other institutions remained committed.

The programme continues to expand and the resources are now included in the National Institute of Teacher Training of the Ministry of Education, making them available to all teachers.

These actions allow a change of view towards a subject that was traditionally considered only by technicians and experts. Teachers act as agents of change, including tax themes in their plans,

María Fernanda Mobilia, Head of Tax Education Division, Community Outreach Directorate, AFIP Argentina

---

Source: OECD Survey on Taxpayer Education Initiatives.

Developing digital resources can help scale up initiatives. The low costs of replication and the increasing availability of IT within schools means that electronic resources can play a useful role in delivering school-based initiatives, enabling common resources to be instantly shared nationally. In Turkey, the Tax Awareness training programme for children seeks to engage children throughout their school career, providing a range of digital resources to support teachers and students. The programme was developed in partnership with the Ministry of National Education, with training materials available through the Ministry's training portal and further materials available on the public website (www.vergibilinci.gov.tr). This has enabled the initiative to reach around 5 million students.

While placing tax on the curriculum is the most comprehensive approach to teaching tax in schools, this is not always (immediately) possible. It can take time and resources to bring tax into the curriculum, both in the tax administration and in schools. Alternative, smaller scale programmes may need to be considered or undertaken as a pilot to prove the value of bringing tax into the school.

Several countries use tax officials to directly deliver lessons to students. For example, in Peru, Japan and Zambia, tax officials (often selected through requests for volunteers) present directly to children, engaging with them in debates and discussing the role of receipts in compliance. While this gives the revenue authority direct control over the content, it makes it more difficult to secure access, with several countries highlighting the challenges of agreeing times with schools. Such programmes are also often limited in scale, as they require the revenue authority to provide the staff. These programmes can, however, be a steppingstone to bringing tax into the curriculum, as shown in Kenya (Box 3.2). A further alternative that may be less resource intensive is for the tax administration to invite children to visit on open days, as happens in Spain and Romania.

Corporate volunteering implemented by SUNAT is an excellent way to strengthen the sense of commitment and conviction with the institutional mission of promoting tax and customs culture in the citizenry.

Marcial Rubén Esquives Guerra, Manager of Tax and Customs Culture, Superintendencia Nacional de Aduanas y de Administración Tributaria (SUNAT), Peru

Competitions and contests provide a way to raise the profile of initiatives and can also be used to encourage students to think about careers in tax. Several countries have contests where students are asked to write essays, letters or presentations on tax. For example, in Japan students write essays on why it is beneficial for everyone to pay taxes; in 2017 over 600 000 essays were submitted by junior high school students. In a contest held since 2008 in Spain, secondary school students have to write a letter to a tax evader, explaining why it is wrong to evade taxes and trying to convince the person to switch behaviour.[1] Tanzania has an annual tax club competition in 311 secondary schools, which includes a competition in fiscal receipt collection, to encourage students and their friends and families to demand receipts when making purchases. Such competitions, often with finalists attending an event in the capital, can generate publicity and help raise the profile of taxpayer education initiatives. The Young Tax Professional of the Year (EY-YPTY) competition, run in many countries (e.g. Malaysia) in collaboration with EY,[2] targets university-level students; it is designed to encourage participants to consider a career in tax. The competition is divided into a preliminary phase – where participants submit a response to a case study via a PowerPoint and a video presentation – and the international final, with students and young graduates representing over 30 countries competing for the EY-YTPY title.

Giving young people an experience of tax administration

While most strategies to engage future taxpayers seek to engage them in their own environment (e.g. school, university), an alternative approach is to bring them into the tax administration. This approach is generally targeted at university students and/or young adults, and seeks to involve them in the tax administration's outreach with the wider population. These programmes generally seek not just to educate the students/young adults participating, but to make them role models, not just during their time in the official programmes, but throughout their working lives.

In Guatemala, 2 500 18–24-year-olds have been included in the "SAT Works for You" initiative. "SAT Works for You" is a civil service programme that the Guatemalan tax administration (Superintendencia de Administración Tributaria, SAT) set up to strengthen ties with the population. Its objectives are to ease taxpayer compliance with tax obligations and regain their trust. This is done by informing citizens about the functioning and importance of SAT in the economic life of the country, promoting tax culture, as well as providing assistance to the Maya-speaking population. The recruits participate in the activities promoting SAT and in the assistance to taxpayers, thus contributing to their communities' development and becoming agents for the spread of tax information. One of the main effects of the SAT programme was the promotion of a better image of the administration among the segments where it was executed.

A similar initiative is deployed by the Mexican SAT, whose aim is to attract university students who are about to start working, providing them with tools to become promoters or spokespersons of tax culture and tax citizenship.

3.1.2. Common challenges and proposed solutions

While there are several different strategies for bringing tax into the curriculum, a set of common challenges has emerged for tax administrations when trying to implement such programmes. This section presents the main obstacles identified and highlights some of the solutions adopted by tax administrations.

Building effective alliances/partnerships (with schools/educational institutions)

It is clear that strong alliances and partnerships are vital, especially to take initiatives to scale, but these can be challenging to build. The most frequent problem highlighted by tax administrations was the reticence of school authorities to devote time and effort to the subject. Several responses to this challenge were identified:

Solution 1- Agreements with local/regional/national governments

Working with the relevant government authorities, ideally to integrate tax into the curriculum, is the most effective and permanent, approach. Obtaining the support of the authorities can enable tax to become part of the mandatory curriculum, unlocking the resources of the education ministries and/or schools to support the teaching of tax. This is the most common partnership observed in the survey. Where there are local/regional authorities, engagement at that level can also help ensure the initiative is implemented in line with local needs and priorities.

Such agreements can take time to develop. In Mauritius, the Mauritius Revenue Authority held several consultative meetings with regulatory bodies and concerned stakeholders to convince them of the importance of introducing tax literacy among the younger generation as a prelude to an agreement to work together.

Solution 2- Working with schools directly

In the absence of formal inclusion in the curriculum, working with schools directly can be effective and can illustrate the value of the initiative. Building relationships with school directors to outline the aims and modalities of the initiative can give the tax authority the opportunity to convince schools of the benefits of teaching tax culture at school. Such an approach generally requires that the tax authority be directly involved in the delivery of the initiative; while this is more resource intensive, it gives the tax authority the opportunity to maintain much greater control and supervision over the implementation of the programme.

Solution 3- Working with educational organisations

In many countries, a range of specialised organisations can help ensure programmes and content are relevant to young people. Tax authorities may not have the skills and up-to-date knowledge and awareness of the tools and trends most likely to engage young people. Partnering with more specialised organisations, especially those working in the education sector, can therefore provide useful assistance to tax administrations in the promotion and implementation of programmes on tax targeting young people, as well as assistance in the preparation and delivery of teaching materials. These can include NGOs as well as student and teacher unions and education institutes. Examples from the survey include the German *Jugend und Bildung*[3], the Mauritius Institute of Education, the Uruguayan National Administration of Public Education and the Spanish Tax Studies Institute, with institutes for education being the most common partners observed in the survey.

Lack of awareness of the programme

Especially when the programme is not officially sponsored by a partner institution, a problem of visibility of the initiative can limit the impact. Several countries reported problems of lack of awareness in their responses to the survey, with several approaches highlighted to address this challenge.

Solution 1- Making materials directly available to teachers

One option is to make it easier for teachers to find and use materials to teach tax. In Germany, the finance ministry has a full range of resources for teachers available on its website. These resources are based on the format/structure teachers are used to and are regularly updated to match the current curriculum.

Solution 2 - Using the provincial branches of the tax administration to promote the initiative across the country

Spreading information on the initiatives throughout the territory is essential and an effective way to enable this is to involve the local branches of the tax administration, as is the case in Spain.

Limited Human Resources

Limited human resources are especially problematic when the initiative requires tax officials to deliver the programme directly (e.g. in schools). The most effective solution to this is to integrate tax into the school curriculum, with teachers delivering the programme; this may require an investment in training the teachers, especially where average societal understanding of tax is limited. Where it is not possible for teachers to deliver the programmes, identifying volunteers among tax officers can be effective. Within the Peruvian SUNAT, for example, the programme attracted the interest of more than 1 000 employees; the level of response was such that it was difficult for SUNAT to accommodate all the requests, yet it enabled the initiative to expand to additional schools.

3.2. Education initiatives for businesses

Many businesses are established by individuals with limited knowledge of how the business tax system works. Addressing this knowledge gap is a key challenge for many countries, especially in the SME sector, where those with responsibility for tax matters may have no experience or qualifications. There are various ways to do this, including providing practical assistance (Chapter 5) or through awareness-raising campaigns (e.g., around filing deadlines – Chapter 4). This section looks at broader initiatives focussed on working substantively and interactively with businesses to build their knowledge and understanding of the tax system through dedicated training/education programmes.

Improving business understanding of the tax system can bring benefits for all. Businesses that are unaware of their obligations and rights run the risk of fines and penalties, as well as potentially not making use of provisions designed to help them. In addition, compliance and enforcement costs for both businesses and tax administrations are likely to be higher when businesses struggle to understand the systems and processes.

Well-designed training programmes for businesses facilitate learning in both directions. The primary focus is to raise the understanding, and ultimately compliance, among businesses regarding their tax affairs. In addition, however, well-designed programmes look to learn from businesses on where to target their efforts, and on how the challenges faced by businesses can be eased by improvements in tax policy and/or administration.

Training on tax can be provided via a range of modalities. These include seminars and face-to-face meetings, as well as webinars categorised by tax issues. Different approaches allow for different combinations of reach and depth of engagement. The best approach will depend on the needs identified and the depth of feedback required from businesses.

3.2.1. Selected policy options

Workshops

Workshops enable detailed and practical education to be provided in specific areas of tax, but significant preparation is needed to maximise their impact. As face-to-face workshops are resource-intensive and can reach a limited number of people/businesses, ensuring that workshops are focussed on the right topics and participants is important.

Consultation with taxpayers and research on taxpayer behaviour can provide valuable inputs into workshop programme design. Consultation with taxpayers provides an opportunity for them to describe what they feel they need from taxpayer education. This approach is most effective when taxpayers are already in the tax system, and have some experience with it, and therefore can effectively articulate the issues on which they require further education. Not all needs can be identified by consultation, however, not least, as many taxpayers (or potential taxpayers from the informal sector) may not be aware of/respond to consultation processes. Yet these may be the taxpayers the programme is looking to target. Tax administrations can use their own data to identify issues and sectors to target. For example, the South African Revenue Service (SARS) uses its internal compliance reports to identify which business sectors to prioritise and target according to their tax needs and responsibilities (Box 3.4).

Identifying the right participants and managing their expectations requires effective communications. While many participants may self-select for participation, others will need more active targeting. For self-selecting participants, making the process as simple as possible is important. In Chile, the Servicio de Impuestos Internos (SII) allows workshops to be booked online, with the website enabling participants to search the range of courses by theme. While this has been successful, an internal evaluation identified a need to include greater specificity in descriptions to ensure that participants attend sessions at the right level for their experience. Where specific taxpayers are being targeted for participation, a clear strategy can be beneficial, identifying the best means of reaching the targets (e.g., through direct communication with taxpayers, social media, traditional media, and industry bodies).

Effective partnerships can help improve the reach and impact of programmes. There range of partnerships observed in business workshop programmes highlights the range of ways in which partnerships can contribute to such programmes. At the more practical end, partnering with educational establishments can help provide locations for workshops, especially when looking to deliver workshops in more remote regions. Partnerships with industry/stakeholder bodies can be especially important to build both relationships and trust. Especially when dealing with businesses that are informal or uncompliant, where there can be fear and mistrust of the tax administration, the involvement of a more trusted group can help encourage participation. For example, in Mauritius workshops are delivered in partnership with groups including the Small Shop Owners Association, the SME Federation and the Women's Entrepreneur Association.

The talks must be classified by the needs of the taxpayers. Consulting the taxpayers themselves is an important source of learning, since considering their needs allows the generation of content that can better meet their expectations.

Mr. Jorge Guzmán, Former Head of Education and Dissemination, Directorate of Taxpayer's Assistance, SII, Chile,

Box 3.4. South Africa: SARS-tailored education workshops

The SARS approach to providing tailored education workshops is twofold. On the one hand, SARS contacts targeted companies to invite them to education sessions; on the other, the various stakeholders, such as companies or government agencies, can also ask SARS for personalised assistance. SARS offers several kinds of education sessions:

- in-house workshops where taxpayers are invited through text messages and the quarterly published schedules on the SARS website
- external workshops on the premises of the stakeholder/industry, based on the requirements specified and on the memorandum of understanding between the respective industries and Taxpayer Education
- tax education sessions given by tax educators who approach stakeholders to offer their services, in return receiving on-site resolutions on their taxpayers.

The workshops incorporate Value Added Tax, Small Business Corporations, Income Tax, Provisional Tax, Pay As You Earn, and Public Benefit Organisations, among other topics.

SARS has collaborated, in the framework of this initiative, with banking establishments – which seek to educate business owners about how to utilize loans acquired from banks – and mining companies whose employees would qualify to receive shares from the company, and who would require education regarding the tax liability upon receipt of their dividends.

Source: OECD Survey on Taxpayer Education Initiatives.

Webinars

Webinars offer opportunities to provide programmes efficiently but can limit the scope for direct feedback and engagement by taxpayers. Many countries report using webinars as either an alternative or a supplement to face-to-face workshops, highlighting their potential for greater reach. For example, British Her Majesty's Revenue and Customs (HMRC) webinars can accommodate up to 1 000 participants, this also limits the opportunity for individuals to ask questions or raise specific challenges with the tax authority. As such, webinars, especially large-scale ones, may be more suited to general introductory programmes than to detailed technical issues. It is also vital that webinars provide details of where taxpayers can obtain further information or support if needed. In this respect, webinars can be a useful complement to more technical workshops, providing a simple, easily accessible introduction and a gateway for more detailed programmes for those who require them.

Effective research on the topics to be covered is even more important for webinars. The restrictions on personal interaction in webinars reduce the scope to adapt or adjust content on delivery. Several of the survey respondents highlighted the importance of surveying taxpayers to identify the topics to cover.

Webinars can use a variety of communication channels to maximise reach. While government websites may be the most obvious place to host/share webinars, they may not be as effective as video hosting sites, such as YouTube, or social networks in reaching the target audience. Especially where programmes are looking to educate those who are less familiar with the tax system, making it easy to find content away from government websites is an important consideration.

Webinars can have a much longer lifespan than workshops and can be edited to make them more accessible. A key advantage of webinars is that once recorded, they can be uploaded for re-watching and therefore can have a much longer lifespan than a one-off workshop. Investing in editing to make the webinar more accessible, for example through the addition of subtitles and/or translation may be an effective investment.

Tax dialogues

Tax dialogues between the revenue authority and taxpayers focus more explicitly on two-way education. While all the workshops highlight the value of feedback (3.4 Impacts), tax dialogues between the revenue authority and businesses have feedback from taxpayers as a primary aim, looking to deepen understanding on both sides.

Whereas traditional workshops place the emphasis on increasing knowledge, tax dialogues focus more on tax morale. In Rwanda, the Commissioner General has regular tax dialogues with the business community in each province; a similar scheme has recently started in Sierra Leone (Box 3.5). In contrast to all other initiatives in this section, which were identified as primarily focussing on increasing the knowledge of taxpayers, tax dialogues focus on building the perception that taxpayers are treated fairly, and on increasing tax morale. In Tanzania, stakeholder forums are organised at the regional level to respond to specific identified needs (Box 3.6).

Box 3.5. Tax dialogues in Rwanda and Sierra Leone

The Rwandan Tax Dialogues is a platform that brings the Rwanda Revenue Authority (RRA) Commissioner General in closer engagement with the business community to identify issues, challenges and possible solutions.

The dialogues take place in each province of Rwanda, as well as the capital, and are organised in partnership with the provincial governor and private sector federations. The Tax Dialogues provide for a two-way exchange, which the RRA perceives as helping build trust among taxpayers, increasing their confidence that they will be treated fairly. It also provides valuable feedback for RRA management on the views and concerns of the business community.

While the programme is estimated to have reached up to 1 500 taxpayers, there remains a challenge in ensuring the engagement of the business community, which is not as high as desired.

In Sierra Leone, there have been two sets of Business Dialogue meetings, organised with the support of the United Nations Development Programme and the African Development Bank. One hosted representatives of large taxpayers, the other small, medium, and micro enterprises.

Feedback from the events showed that taxpayers welcomed the opportunity to provide inputs into the tax administration process. The Sierra Leone National Revenue Authority (NRA) in return has welcomed concrete recommendations from taxpayers on how to improve the tax administration.

Source: OECD Survey on Taxpayer Education Initiatives and Sierra Leone National Revenue Authority.

Box 3.6. Stakeholder forums in Tanzania

Stakeholder forums are regional meetings that bring together the business community with the Tanzania Revenue Authority (TRA). The agenda for the forum is determined through feedback received from call centres, seminars or previous forums, which help to identify the specific needs in the area.

Working with the local TRA office, the forums are widely publicised through local media and planned to be highly participative, combining entertainment together with the technical content to encourage participation.

The Forums provide an opportunity for taxpayers to engage with the TRA, not only to gain information but also to raise concerns/complaints as well as provide feedback to the TRA to help improve their service and set the agenda for future Forums.

Source: Tanzania Revenue Authority.

3.2.2. Common challenges and proposed solutions

The main challenges encountered by those tax administrations having implemented education initiatives for businesses appear to be organisational and infrastructural in nature. The challenges are mainly associated with identifying the right participants, as well as the logistics for running the programmes. Effective research on taxpayer needs and flexibility in implementation appear to be the main solutions adopted.

Heterogeneity of targets

A common challenge is the wide variety of participant knowledge and needs. Effective research and preparation, combined with targeted communications to ensure that the desired participants attend, can help address this challenge. Many countries reported the value of using surveys to identify priorities for workshops/webinars, while others highlighted the role of tax administration data in identifying high-risk taxpayers to target. Creating feedback loops, so feedback from one workshop improves the design and targeting of subsequent workshops, has also been stressed by some countries. Providing follow-up resources, including footage of the workshop itself, can help ensure that participants who struggle to keep up during the workshop are able to reinforce their learning.

Encouraging participation

Encouraging participation can be challenging, especially when non-compliant taxpayers are being targeted. Countries identified a variety of approaches, including using social media networks, advertising on local radio, and direct contact by letter and/or email with high-risk taxpayers. Partnerships with trade bodies can help too, not least as these may reduce fear of engaging with the tax administration. In cases where trust of the tax administration is low, it may even be worth encouraging trade bodies or other groups to run education programmes independently. Some countries also provide a certificate of completion, which may help incentivise participation.

Integrating tax compliance into a broader programme to support business development may make initiatives more appealing. In Indonesia, the Business Development Services programme provides a broad curriculum to support micro, small and medium enterprises. Co-ordinated by the Ministry of Economic Affairs, it is run in partnership with several other ministries and covers issues such as branding, digital marketing and exporting, as well as bookkeeping and taxation.[4]

Logistical issues

Logistical issues, such as difficulties in finding suitable venues and getting digital novices to register online, can lessen the impact of programmes. Partnerships with universities or local municipalities can help address the challenges of finding venues; in some cases, seminars are even provided directly in the offices of the companies requesting support. For countries where digital participation is not yet the norm, introducing online access to education can be challenging. Providing clear and simple instructions tested with the target audience is an obvious and effective solution. Several countries also identified a challenge, for both the tax administration and companies, in finding the right schedules for workshops and webinars; the ability to watch on demand is a potential solution to this problem, but does result in limited feedback.

3.3. Education initiatives for individuals

In addition to their needs to be educated on their rights and responsibilities on paying taxes, individuals also often require education or information to enable them to hold governments (of all levels) accountable for how their taxes are raised and spent. While there are various examples of support provided to individuals on their rights and responsibilities for paying taxes, there are far fewer examples of support in holding governments to account. In part, this may be because the tax administrations may not see this clearly as part of their responsibilities. There are, however, other organisations that do focus on supporting individuals in this area, especially civil society organisations; the role of civil society organisations and other non-governmental actors will be covered in more detail in Chapter 6.

Given these dual needs, the initiatives to support individuals can take various forms and involve different actors. A wide range of initiatives were reported in the survey, including workshops for taxpayers (Lithuania) and monthly meetings with taxpayers (Romania). These are similar to initiatives undertaken for businesses, and so are not covered in detail in this section. Initiatives uniquely for individuals include programmes aimed at vulnerable groups, (e.g. Canada's Outreach Programme, Box 3.7 and Argentina's fiscal assistant programme), as well as initiatives that work with civil society organisations (e.g. Sierra Leone, Box 3.8).

One common objective of many initiatives aimed at educating individuals is the demystification of the tax administration. Many individuals, especially more vulnerable taxpayers, can find the tax administration confusing or even intimidating. Many initiatives are seeking to reduce this fear and confusion, making individuals more willing to both pay taxes and seek further support, including practical assistance of the type covered in Chapter 5. In Guatemala, the Tax Awareness Programme works with taxpayers who have been given suspended criminal sentences, in addition to encouraging participants to consider the consequences of their actions on tax collection (and subsequently state services), the programme also seeks to inform them regarding how the tax administration works, including differences between administrative and criminal offences.

Some of the initiatives combine both in-depth dialogue through teaching-focussed initiatives, such as those described in this chapter, with the more high-level communication-focussed initiatives of Chapter 4. This is especially true in initiatives focussed on supporting vulnerable groups, where a more intensive approach may be needed to ensure effective communication. Such initiatives have been included in this chapter due to their commonalities with other initiatives in the chapter that look to provide a greater depth of engagement and encourage feedback to the tax administration.

3.3.1. Selected policy options

Outreach programmes for vulnerable taxpayers

Vulnerable taxpayers may rely on their tax returns to establish eligibility for benefits and credits, which can increase the importance of providing education. In many countries, government benefits and credits are linked to information provided on personal income tax returns. This can make it especially important that vulnerable populations, including seniors, refugees and people with disabilities, are willing and able to participate in the tax system, which is why some countries have specific programmes designed to engage with them.

Because vulnerable taxpayers may be especially difficult to reach by the revenue authority, partnerships with dedicated community groups can be important. Many vulnerable groups may have limited experience with or confidence in engaging with the state and may not actively seek out support from the revenue authority. Partnerships with community groups with established relationships with the target populations can therefore help. One example of this approach is the Canadian Revenue Agency (CRA) Outreach Programme (Box 3.7).

Box 3.7. Canada: Outreach Programme

The Canada Revenue Agency (CRA) Outreach Programme centres on increasing awareness and education related to benefit and credit entitlements available to Canada's more vulnerable populations (indigenous peoples, newcomers and refugees, seniors, youth and students, people with disabilities, homeless and housing-insecure individuals, and modest-income Canadians), as well as providing them with information on benefits and credits.

The CRA employs dedicated outreach officers across the regions; they provide year-round, in-person presentations to these individuals and the community organisations that support them. During in-person visits, the outreach officers support individuals by telling them about the documents they might need when they receive a letter from the CRA. Outreach officers also promote the CRA's Community Volunteer Income Tax Programme (CVITP) (Chapter 5), through which community organisations host free tax preparation clinics and arrange for volunteers to complete income tax and benefit returns for eligible individuals who have a modest income and a simple tax situation.

Through the Outreach Programme, organisations that serve vulnerable segments can schedule an in-person visit from an outreach officer. CRA outreach officers may present an information session for employees or clients, host a booth, or deliver a presentation at an event; they also provide tailored products to help inform individuals about tax-filing topics. These visits are conducted year-round (not just during tax season) and allow the CRA to reach vulnerable segments of the population – including those in remote communities.

The Outreach Programme also works with schools, shelters, settlement organisations, Indigenous organisations, professional associations, seniors' groups, organisations supporting disabled people, and provincial and municipal governments to promote and host outreach events, leveraging their networks to increase the reach of CRA messaging. In addition, since 2016 the programme has collaborated with Service Canada, providing joint outreach to Indigenous communities. In response to the Covid-19 pandemic, activities have become virtual, enabling access to continue.

The main challenges in the programme have been adapting to the needs of the target communities by finding better ways to reach them and tailoring the materials in terms of both their content and their provision in languages beyond the two official languages of Canada.

In 2017 the programme reached over 73 000 individuals, with the equivalent of 55 full time employees working directly in the programme.

Source: OECD Survey on Taxpayer Education Initiatives.

Embedding taxpayer education in broader civil society programmes

Civil society organisations supporting the economic development of their communities can be useful partners in taxpayer education. Embedding taxpayer education in civil society programmes cannot only help reach a larger audience, but also help taxpayers see how tax compliance sits within the broader economic development of the community. Sierra Leone's NRA partnership with the Civil Society Consortium is one example of how such partnerships can work (Box 3.8)

Box 3.8. Sierra Leone's partnership with the Civil Society Consortium

The Civil Society Consortium (CSC) is made up of mostly non-governmental organisations that help communities in addressing their socio-economic challenges. These organisations are respected and have authority in the local communities. Therefore, they get a good audience among the leaders and members of communities in the interior towns and villages. They use the local radio stations and town criers to engage with people and disseminate information.

With the intent of improving tax education in the country and to get members of the public to see the NRA as a partner in the development of the country, collaboration with these organisations was sought for tax education and promotion of voluntary compliance in areas that may not have been reached due to resource limitations. The Consortium members accompany the staff of the NRA to give more voice to messages and education on media platforms while they go on their own to villages for town hall meetings.

This was the first time the NRA signed a memorandum of understanding with a non-governmental organisation as part of its taxpayer education work. The NRA found that this partnership helped improve the public perception of the NRA, which had previously been associated mostly with enforcement, rather than helping taxpayers with their challenges. The project ran successfully, but a renewal has been postponed due to Covid-19.

Main challenge:

The members of the consortium were trained well by tax officers, but there are some tax issues they could not address in detail. They therefore had to ask taxpayers to contact the NRA when there was no staff member with them during a tax education programme.

Solution:

The NRA asked tax officers closer to the area where the consortium is engaging in tax education initiatives to join them, or it provided staff contact numbers when some taxpayers' enquiries were difficult to address.

Source: OECD Survey on Taxpayer Education Initiatives.

3.3.2. Common challenges and proposed solutions for implementation

Geographic reach

As many of the communities being targeted are geographically dispersed, both use of online resources and local partners can help. While online resources may be easier to arrange, especially when targeting vulnerable populations, IT proficiency should not be assumed; online access should also not always be assumed, especially in developing countries. Identifying partners who can help extend the reach is therefore vital for some programmes.

Human resources

Programmes engaging individuals can be very resource-intensive; partnerships can reduce the demand on revenue-authority staff, allowing them to focus where the expertise is most needed. Most revenue authorities do not have the number of staff needed for mass campaigns. Lithuania's ability to deliver workshops, for example, is in part limited by the number of staff trained to deliver the programme. Working with, and training, partners who can provide the basic teaching on taxes can be beneficial, enabling more complex and detailed questions to filter through to the tax authority, as seen in Sierra Leone. Other approaches include providing flexibility to allow staff from across the revenue authority to volunteer to participate, as done in Argentina (Box 3.9), helping to increase resources.

Box 3.9. Argentina: Fiscal Assistant Programme

The Fiscal Assistant Programme in Argentina seeks to engage vulnerable groups in the tax system. It does this by seeking to engage with such individuals in the community, where the atmosphere is likely to be more relaxed and the tax administration will appear less threatening. The initiative is organised in partnership with local authorities to help ensure access to spaces where the tax administration is usually not present.

All employees of the tax administration are permitted to volunteer to become fiscal assistants and receive training to enable them to participate in the programme. Initially, there were challenges in ensuring that fiscal assistants would be permitted to take time away from their usual duties to participate in the programme; new procedures were required to facilitate the process. High-level support from the Federal Administrator helped encourage managers to support the programme.

While the programme remains in its early stages, early results have been promising and there are discussions to expand the programme. In common with other initiatives of this type, the employees delivering the programme have noted its value in providing feedback to enable them to improve the performance of their usual duties.

Source: OECD Survey on Taxpayer Education Initiatives.

Trust

Allying with grassroots organisations allows more effective outreach and legitimacy in the eyes of the public, which is sometimes accustomed to the presence of such organisations on the territory. Such partnerships can therefore be essential in allowing programmes to reach their target audience. Chapter 6 discusses in more detail the role of non-governmental organisations in taxpayer education.

3.4. Impacts

Especially in the case of the initiatives targeting future taxpayers, the initiatives in this chapter are likely to have a significant lag between the delivery of the initiative and its impact on taxpayer behaviour. In many cases, and even more so where younger children are targeted, it may be many years before any increase in tax morale in individuals will be realised. This makes it especially difficult to track the impact of such programmes on behaviour, as demonstrated by the lack of in-depth impact assessments in the responses to the survey.

Qualitative assessments of initiatives are possible, with many programmes showing high satisfaction levels. Several countries have reported undertaking some assessment of their initiatives, generally focussed on the evaluation of the classes being taught and/or the dedicated materials produced. While such surveys may not be able to track the ultimate impact of the initiatives, they provide valuable feedback on how effective the materials created are as teaching instruments, as well as on how to improve the delivery of courses. In both the United Kingdom (UK) and Germany, participants in webinars surveyed indicated positive results. In the UK, the webinars delivered in 2018/19 had a customer satisfaction score of 88.81%. In Germany, the Federal Ministry of Finance surveyed secondary school teachers participating in their initiative, with 94% being highly satisfied with the teaching materials and 85% reporting that they were using the materials in other classes beyond the initiative.

Surveys can also generate valuable feedback to improve the design of initiatives. In Greece, the Independent Authority for Public Revenue's Directorate of Tax Compliance undertook a survey which highlighted the individual teaching style and the technical infrastructure available in the schools as the key factors. Furthermore, it identified differences of opinions: primary school teachers thought that the tax education programme should be included in an already existing module, while junior high and high school teachers believed it would be better taught autonomously in the form of a project or as group assignments.

Short-term impacts on both knowledge and perceptions have been identified from some programmes. While the long-term impacts on tax compliance may be difficult to track, it is possible to assess the short-term impact on participants in terms of what they learned through the initiatives. Slovenia undertakes surveys on attitudes towards tax, which are compared between those students who have taken part in the initiative and those who have not. The results indicate strongly that those who participated had a more positive attitude toward and awareness of tax than those who did not participate.

Taxpayer workshops identified positive impacts in the relationships with the tax authority. In Senegal, workshops of around 60 SMEs were organised in each fiscal district. The evaluation highlighted that while most of those participating, especially from the informal sector, had a pre-existing fear of the tax authority, following the workshops there was near unanimous acceptance of the legitimacy of the tax authority and a widespread commitment to increase compliance.

[These workshops] show that a large proportion of taxpayers, especially those in the informal sector, have a fear of the tax administration, fuelled by ignorance and lack of tax culture. At the end of the workshops, they are almost unanimous in affirming the validity of the tax system and in committing to greater compliance with their tax obligations.

Alain Paul Sene, Head of Quality and Communications Office, General Directorate of Taxes and Government Property (DGID), Senegal

---

In addition, all the workshop-style initiatives highlighted the value of feedback from participants both in improving the specific initiative, and in highlighting broader challenges for participants in engaging with the tax system. In many cases (e.g. Rwanda, Box 3.5, and Argentina, Box 3.9) the feedback highlighted additional needs for more detailed/practical support for specific participants. The recognition of the value and impact of the feedback suggests that effective feedback mechanisms should be an integral part of workshop-style initiatives.

References

OECD (2019), *Tax Morale: What Drives People and Businesses to Pay Tax?*, OECD Publishing, Paris, https://dx.doi.org/10.1787/f3d8ea10-en. [1]

Notes

[1] https://www.agenciatributaria.es/AEAT.internet/Inicio/La_Agencia_Tributaria/Educacion_Civico_Tributaria/Concurso_nacional_de_redaccion_2018/Concurso_nacional_de_redaccion_2018.shtml.

[2] https://www.ey.com/my/en/careers/students/young-tax-professional-of-the-year#fragment-3-na.

[3] https://jugend-und-bildung.de/beratung/.

4 Communicating tax to raise awareness

This chapter presents initiatives aimed at communicating tax to raise awareness. It illustrates how information campaigns can be used to communicate tax effectively. It also presents initiatives that help to build a strong and positive relationship between tax administrations and taxpayers, as well as those focussed on reaching specific groups of people.

There is no one way to reach out to taxpayers to raise awareness about tax. This is why tax administrations use a wide range of actions. Many tax administrations have launched programmes to inform taxpayers of specific issues and deadlines. They have also created or participated in initiatives aimed at getting in touch with taxpayers at specific locations, such as fairs, or even reaching them at home through TV shows or magazines. To avoid ignoring taxpayers who cannot be reached through these channels and to deliver specific messages, tax administrations have also created communication plans, sometimes with the participation of academics and scholars.

Whereas Chapter 3 looked at initiatives that were focussed on intensive and in-depth engagement with taxpayers, building dialogue and/or a deeper understanding of the tax system, this chapter looks at awareness-raising initiatives. While there is inevitably some overlap between the two, it seems useful to make a distinction between the initiatives in Chapter 3, which are generally focussed more on teaching methodologies or building dialogue with the tax administration, and the initiatives in this chapter, which are more focussed on communication to raise awareness among taxpayers of what is happening in the field of taxation around them.

Further details on 53 of the initiatives analysed to inform this chapter can be found in Annex A.

4.1. Information campaigns

As the tax system relies on voluntary compliance, it is important to ensure sufficient awareness of the laws, including any changes. As initiatives that essentially advertise the tax system are potentially a useful tool, some of the most common ones were reported in this survey. Predominately using mass media, such as TV or radio, Internet (including social media), direct contact and publications, such initiatives convey messages to a wide range of taxpayers.

While most "advertising" campaigns focus on tax laws, some – especially those focussing on the informal sector – take a different approach. Raising awareness of the societal benefits of public spending enabled by tax is an aspect highlighted by some initiatives. In several countries, the targets of campaigns for formalisation are not informal businesses directly, but rather their customers in an effort to change their behaviour by demanding tax receipts, thereby forcing sellers to adapt. When people avoid buying goods from the informal sector, sellers start to comply with tax laws.

4.1.1. Selected policy options

Improving taxpayer knowledge by disseminating information to the largest audience possible

Taxpayers are often unaware of their rights and obligations. In Africa, difficulty in accessing information about taxes has been found to be correlated with a lower willingness to pay taxes (OECD, 2019[1]); in such cases, mass information campaigns may be a useful tool to help build tax morale. Tax administrations can use information campaigns to inform taxpayers of the general tax codes or update them on new tax legislation. Such campaigns can use one or more of a variety of communication mediums, for example they can engage with taxpayers through social networks and call centres, explaining what taxes are for and how they are spent.

Campaigns can be run on general tax compliance issues as well as on particular pieces of legislation that are either new or that generally see a low compliance rate. This was the case, for instance, in Israel, where the Israel Tax Authority (ITA) ran a campaign to nudge taxpayers to comply with new legislation prohibiting the use of cash for certain payments and transactions, in force as of 2019. The campaign was launched in December 2018 and encompassed material diffused through radio, TV, the Internet, press and social media. Moreover, it included billboards and meetings with the bureaus of tax representatives. Before the campaign was launched and funded – in late November – the ITA conducted interviews and provided write-ups in the media.

TV and radio programmes are also a useful means to reach out to different categories of taxpayers. Some administrations, like the Tanzania Revenue Authority and the National Revenue Authority of Sierra Leone, use both national and local radio and TV channels to maximise the impacts. National channels are used for more generic taxpayer information or announcements and advertisements that apply to the majority of taxpayers, while local radios are used to reach out to specific taxpayers in a region or district. As shown in the following section, these media can also be used to improve the image of tax administrations.

Increasing compliance by explaining the use of money collected

Apart from obligations, it is also important that tax administrations highlight how taxes are spent and distributed. Showing taxpayers the social utility of taxes can help change their perceptions about tax, which too often overemphasise the costs while dismissing the benefits. For them to adopt a more co-operative behaviour, citizens must be aware that contributing to taxes benefits every citizen – including themselves. The French Ministries for Economy and Finance, and its Public Action and Accounts have dedicated a section on their website (www.economie.gouv.fr) to explaining the benefits and the use made of taxpayer monies: *À quoi servent mes impôts?*[1] (What are my taxes for?).

Apart from creating a dedicated website, it is also possible to annex such information to tax returns or to include it in larger initiatives, for instance within an information campaign. The message can take many forms, such as graphs or texts, but is most efficient when taxpayers can relate to it. For instance, as in Ivory Coast (see image below), it may be useful to explain what it represents in terms of infrastructure such as hospitals, schools, etc.

Figure 4.1. Ivory Coast: Linking taxes and tangible benefits

Source: DGI Côte d'Ivoire

The less taxpayers trust the government and its institutions, the more crucial it is to provide them with this kind of information, as it can create a sense of accountability. It is thus important to repeat the messages as often as possible, using as many channels as possible.

Tackling the informal sector by changing behaviour among the general public

To increase tax compliance and tackle the informal sector, tax administrations can reach out to taxpayers through a range of campaigns, which constitute alternative ways of communicating with

them to ensure that they adopt beneficial behaviour – for instance encouraging them to control that shops and stores produce invoices, to pay their taxes on time and to adopt taxpayer identification numbers.

The types of campaigns vary and can include means of incentivising people to adopt desirable behaviour. This is for instance the case where collecting receipts can lead to a tax deduction or the participation in lotteries (Box 4.1). For instance, the Lithuanian tax administration (STI) put in place a National Receipt Lottery targeting the riskiest categories of taxpayers (restaurants, car services, spa centres and marketplaces). Portugal's Tax and Customs Authority (TCA) organised a Lucky Invoice Draw to promote tax compliance, inform citizens and tackle tax evasion and fraud. This lottery awards prizes, at random, to customers who have purchased goods or services within the national territory and have requested the issuance of invoices with their TIN (taxpayer identification number).

In such cases, the main goal is not only to inform taxpayers about rules or deadlines, but also to convince them of the power of acting collectively. These campaigns aim to reach the widest audience possible and to reduce the informal sector in an indirect way: by having taxpayers/consumers do what tax administrations are not able to do, i.e., check thousands of receipts in a very large number of places over a limited span of time.

Box 4.1. Slovenia: Motivating taxpayers to check invoices

To support the implementation of certified cash registers, introduced in 2016, the Financial Administration of the Republic of Slovenia (FARS) launched, in partnership with the Government Communication Office and the Slovenian Lottery, a crowd-sourcing campaign to engage citizens in the reduction of the shadow economy and crack down on invoice fraud. To motivate citizens to ask for invoices, FARS launched a lottery called "Use your head: Demand a receipt!". Participants had to collect at least ten receipts, check them and send them to FARS.

The lottery was implemented alongside the launch of the "Check your receipt" app, through which taxpayers who wanted to participate had to register with their tax number. The Government Communication Office assisted FARS in advertising and communication via social media.

When preparing the campaign, FARS highlighted three key threats that could have been potential obstacles to its implementation. First, FARS was aware of not being a popular authority among the public because of the nature of its work, which could constitute an obstacle in motivating citizens to verify invoices on a voluntary basis. Second, consumers and media could see the campaign as a way of denouncing or snitching on entrepreneurs or companies. Third, the fact that FARS was spending taxpayers' money on the campaign, and especially on the prizes, could be seen in a bad light. All these risks were resolved with the help of a positive campaign, where FARS, rather than using an argument of force and power (a "stick"), used a carrot instead.

Impact

In just one year of the campaign, taxpayers have checked more than 21 million invoices. Considering that Slovenia has two million inhabitants, in one year this was equivalent to every Slovenian checking and sending ten invoices to the Financial Administration. In 2016, 112 887 consumers (5.6% of Slovenia's population) downloaded the application (*Preveri račun*) on their mobile phones to check invoices and participate in the competition. In one year, the invoices of 75% of users of certified cash registers were checked at least once. In other words, consumers used their mobile phones to check three-quarters of all issuers of invoices using certified cash registers.

These results can be compared with the costs of the campaign: EUR 200 000 for advertising, prizes and production.

Source: OECD Survey on Taxpayer Education Initiatives.

4.1.2. **Effective mass communication on tax: Common challenges and proposed solutions**

Covering a large part of the population could be a challenge, but most of the tax administrations overcame it by mixing different channels of communication. One of many examples is the Irish communication programmes (Box 4.2). Another option is to run several campaigns each year, as was the case for the Malaysian tax administration.

Changing people's perceptions of tax is not an easy task. The most successful initiatives implemented by tax administrations are those that do not only inform taxpayers about their rights and duties but do so in an innovative way. This can entail providing reasons why taxpayers are better off paying taxes, apart from highlighting the possibility of incurring sanctions. This may include using alternative means of communication and adopting a more personal approach, such as personal letters and visits, as well as organising campaigns to motivate tax compliance, such as lotteries and outreach programmes.

Box 4.2. Ireland: Revenue Commissioners communication programmes

Since 2016, the Irish Office of Revenue Commissioners ("Revenue") has run comprehensive communication programmes targeting individual and newly registered taxpayers. In addition to assisting them in complying with their tax requirements, the campaign sought to help them gain a better understanding of taxes in general, as well as to discover where to find useful information using the website and the Revenue Online Service (ROS) Technical Help Centre.

This initiative comprised a general media campaign, additional self-help guidance on the website, and pamphlets for or direct contact with specific cohorts of taxpayers. The key messages included reminders of deadlines, explanations of how to use the ROS and information on how to benefit from an extended deadline for online filing and paying.

Revenue produced a range of short instructional videos on the Revenue Ireland YouTube channel to show how to register for ROS and how to file income tax returns online. These videos have proved to be an essential element of Revenue's communication and marketing campaign, resulting in positive feedback. To date, the video on how to register for ROS has been viewed more than 28 000 times.

Additionally, Revenue identified and contacted cohorts of taxpayers (for example, newly registered, those with agents and those who filed paper returns) to remind them about their obligations, promote online filing (including access to prefilled tax returns) and advise them of website guidance and videos. The information was summarised for representative and sectoral bodies, such as farmers' organisations, property owner bodies and bodies supporting new businesses.

From 2016 to date, the Pay and File campaigns have proven very successful according to a number of criteria. The volume of phone calls in the run-up to annual filing deadlines was reduced year after year, an increasing number of taxpayers downloaded prefilled tax returns, and in 2018, for the first time, more than 0.5m online income tax returns were filed. Furthermore, a survey of self-employed individuals highlighted that 63% were aware of the videos. They also reported high satisfaction levels regarding the information on the website, saying that the videos, guidelines and phone contacts had proved to be invaluable.

Source: OECD Survey on Taxpayer Education Initiatives.

Below are the two most common challenges encountered by tax administrations in the implementation of measures aimed at informing taxpayers and explaining tax to them, together with some successful strategies to overcome them.

Delivering a clear message

Language plays a crucial role in these types of interactions with taxpayers, as it can make complex issues easy to understand.

Solution 1 – User journeys

The Norwegian Tax Administration (NTA) and the Canada Revenue Agency (CRA) adapted to the different needs of their customers by creating user journeys – which help visualise the optimal interaction between the tax administration and taxpayers – and testing the usability of their services with representatives from the target audiences. In this way, for example, the NTA succeeded in:

- giving certain sub-sets of taxpayers, such as foreigners, the information they needed
- carrying out risk-assessment procedures
- simplifying and adapting the contents of its website and publications aimed at the selected group
- carrying out campaigns aimed at the target audience in tax offices and online, including on social media.

Solution 2 – Simple messages

Avoiding jargon and using simple and plain language is key; for this reason, it is important to work in close contact with the tax administration's communication team or external partners. The provision of access to legal codes and laws can efficiently be complemented by targeted guides, tailored to the needs of taxpayers. For instance, in Morocco the tax administration is present on a wide range of social media and interacts with citizens on a daily basis, publishing videos and posts explaining, in simple language, new developments in tax as well as taxpayer rights and duties. In Canada, the CRA has made a commitment to using plain language and has revised its communications accordingly. In Greece, a wide range of guides is published to inform and assist taxpayers.

> *The creation of useful guides is in the context of co-operative compliance. The central axis is to strengthen the relations between tax administration and taxpayers, with the triple commitment of the tax administration to the latter for transparency, accessibility and responsiveness.*
>
> Mr. KATSIPIS Ioannis, Director, Directorate of Tax Compliance, Independent Authority for Public Revenue (IAPR), Greece

---

Generating public support

For information campaigns to be successful, taxpayers need to engage with them and take appropriate actions. This may prove difficult, as taxes may not be their primary concern.

Solution 1 – Friendly approaches

Friendly approaches are very efficient at achieving a positive attitude among taxpayers. An important element to remember when interacting with taxpayers is that using arguments of force and authority might backfire in terms of encouraging voluntary contribution.

Solution 2 – Incentives

Several countries have sought to incentivise desirable behaviour. As shown in Box 4.1, the Slovenian tax administration used a lottery to motivate people to check invoices, which proved efficient according to the results of this initiative.

4.2. Building a strong and positive relationship with taxpayers

A strong and positive relationship with taxpayers is the goal of many tax administrations. In Africa, a more positive perception of the legitimacy of the tax administration was identified as having the largest correlation with willingness to pay tax (OECD, 2019[11]). Many tax administrations are thus seeking to use communication campaigns to shift perceptions of the tax system, going further than single-issue campaigns. Lotteries, for instance, catch the attention of taxpayers; nonetheless, they focus only on a single issue and may not retain attention for a long time.

One way to build a long-lasting and positive relationship with taxpayers is to be present in their daily lives. This can be done through TV programmes broadcasted before or after the evening news, or through magazines edited to present tax issues in a playful and simple way.

Organising events around the theme of tax citizenship is also a common way to promote compliance, especially during the tax filing season. These events, usually annual, are good opportunities for tax administrations to gather key stakeholders and deliver messages to them in a positive and enjoyable manner. This often implies organising recreational activities for children and their parents, providing information and assistance to taxpayers while demonstrating availability. These events are opportunities to celebrate compliant taxpayers and thank officials of tax administrations, and they offer a time and place for open discussions about tax matters.

4.2.1. Selected policy options

Being closer to taxpayers

Making tax part of day-to-day life can help taxpayers feel closer to tax administrations and make officials seem more approachable and understanding. In several countries, mostly in Africa, tax administrations design TV shows dedicated to taxes (Box 4.3).

Box 4.3. Senegal: A regular TV show designed and presented by tax officials

Senegal's General Directorate of Taxes and Government Property (DGID) broadcasts a TV Show – called "La Minute DGID" – on Radiodifusion Télévision Sénégalaise, the main public TV channel. The programme is aired twice every Monday: first in Wolof, the main national language, at 7:30 p.m. after the main edition of the news bulletin in this language; and second in French, just after the main edition of the news bulletin in French at 8 p.m.

The moment chosen to air the show makes it possible to reach a very large part of the population at a time when they are home and may be more receptive to the message. To broaden the audience, the content is then posted online on the DGID site.

Every edition of the programme is designed and presented by a tax officer who decides on the content of the broadcast. The tax officer in charge changes every week to allow coverage of a vast array of issues and to spread the burden of preparing for the show among many people. However, the Communication and Quality Office of DGID is always involved, as it oversees the preparation of the supports, the co-ordination of the filming and the validation of the message.

Source: OECD Survey on Taxpayer Education Initiatives.
Image: DGID – Senegal.

Another way to build this kind of relationship is through magazines which can also enter taxpayers' homes, such as the Guinean *Fisc-Info* or the Togolese *OTR Actu*. Once printed and distributed, copies of the magazine may end up in the living room and be read by several members of the household or visiting friends and family. Cartoons are especially useful to interest kids and young adults, as well as to render complex issues simple. They may be found either within the magazine or in specific publications such as

in Nigeria. It is also possible to record messages through regular podcasts, as done by the Indonesia Directorate General of Taxes.

Figure 4.2. Examples of magazines with tax messages

Digital tools are a vital component of education approaches to reach the younger generations. Life is increasingly lived online, especially among the younger generations, and so young people need to be engaged digitally, both to ensure accessibility (especially when initiatives are not integrated into formal schooling) and to help promote tax administration as accessible, modern and technologically advanced.

Tax administrations have been experimenting with a range of innovative digital tools and platforms. The tools can take the form of educational videos on taxes, explaining in a fun and simple way the utility and categories of taxes (for example the UK's Tax Facts videos). Other approaches include web games that show how taxes affect society at large (for example Norway's Spleiselaget (Box 4.4), Finland's Taxcampus and Morocco's Madinati). Web portals that include educational materials for children have also been developed (for example the European Union's TAXEDU portal and the Turkish Vergi Bilinci); several tax administrations have also provided their tools via apps for phones, realising that phones are the primary digital device for many (examples include Morocco's Madinati and the EU's Taxlandia game). The most innovative end of the spectrum includes approaches such as the Norway Tax Administration's YouTube video, "Money Back on the Skætt", where fictional characters rap about tax.

Box 4.4. Norway: The Spleiselaget website, computer game and lecture to fight the informal economy

The Norwegian Tax Administration (Skatteetaten) chose to develop a computer game for pupils in secondary schools to teach them how taxes benefit both themselves as individuals and society as a whole. The game is not only a recreational activity but is also part of a teaching plan and complements a set of exercises that can be used by the teacher in class to make the effect last longer. The game uses second-screen technology, meaning that participants log on to the presentation with their mobile phones and shape the content with the input given.

For example, one of the questions was about the informal economy. The app used to run the presentation makes calculations based on the participants' answers to show them the effect of their answers – both among the specific group of participants and for Norway as a whole. For example, if students were to perform undeclared work for X Norwegian kroner, Norway would lose X% of tax income, which could have been used to fund X people in nursing homes or X pupils in upper secondary school.

The game is realised via a special collaboration called *Samarbeid mot svart økonomi* (working together against the shadow economy); it comprises labour unions and employer's organisations, in addition to the Norwegian Tax Administration, and works to emphasize how undeclared work and the shadow economy affect both employers and employees negatively.

This initiative produced extremely interesting results:

1. A computer game for secondary school, designed to respond to competence aims in several subjects (social studies, math, geography, Norwegian), has been played approximately 50 000 times every year since its release in 2015.
2. A 90-minute lecture for upper secondary school students, also designed to respond to competence aims in several subjects, is given by the Norwegian Tax Administration every year; around 600 "Tax Facts Ambassadors" meet over 40 000 pupils each year.

A website was also created. It can be used alone, or in connection with the computer game or the lecture.

It is estimated that the initiative has reached around 700 000 students since 2014.

Source: OECD Survey on Taxpayer Education Initiatives.

It is vital to update and refresh digital tools. Online trends and technology change quickly and tax administrations need to bear this in mind; it is not only important to ensure that the initial launch of the product will engage the target audience, but also to regularly review digital tools to ensure they continue to engage the target audience.

Organising events to gather taxpayers around tax

The events organised by tax administrations depend on the country and the resources available. While no two events are alike, they often have a lot in common. The three most commonly held are:

- **tax days**, such as the Celebrating Taxpayers' Appreciation Day in Rwanda, the National Taxpayer Day in Sierra Leone, the Tax Day in Indonesia and many others
- **tax weeks**, such as Turkey's Tax Week (Box 4.5)
- **fairs**, such as Bangladesh's Income Tax Fair (Box 4.6)

Those events can be organised at a single location or, more frequently, can take place in numerous venues all around the country. Tax administrations are often structured around local offices, which are often in charge of the local events that constitute the building blocks of a nationwide event.

Box 4.5. Turkey's tax week

Turkey's tax week takes place annually during the last week in February. It aims at enhancing tax awareness among children, taxpayers and citizens at large. During the week, country-wide campaigns are run to convey strong messages inviting citizens to pay their taxes and to help them tackle the informal economy. It involves the participation of 500 tax officials all around the country.

The main aspects are:

- visits to taxpayers at their workplaces to collect their opinions and suggestions
- visits to civil society organisations to collect their opinions and suggestions
- stands at universities providing students with information on tax awareness, the dangers of the informal economy employment, career opportunities, etc.
- seminars at universities
- posters on tax awareness for the general public and children.

Source: OECD Survey on Taxpayer Education Initiatives.

Different types of engagements can take place between tax administrations and taxpayers during such events. The main advantage is that they provide a friendly environment that promotes open discussion. They may be designed for audiences such as children and parents, or for more specific audiences such as entrepreneurs.

The most common offer of activities comprise:

- **presentations by high-level government officials** (such as ministers) explaining their perception of the country and the role taxation plays
- **awarding of prizes** to compliant taxpayers and outstanding officials
- **exchanges** with taxpayers in a friendly atmosphere
- **distribution of flyers and publications** produced by the tax administration
- **activities** such as contests or games for children.

These events are short but compared to other initiatives their preparation may require important time and resources. Tax administrations bear all the risks and costs related to organising these events. Officials need to spend a significant amount of time planning, organising and implementing them. Logistical costs may be important, depending on the country and the agenda. Some countries, such as Bangladesh, devote important resources to these events (Box 4.6). Other examples of tax events of this type include Burundi's National Taxpayer Day, Senegal's National Information Days and the Guatemalan Citizen Culture Festival, "Strength Lies in Numbers".

Box 4.6. Bangladesh: The National Board of Revenue's tax events and fair

Every year, Bangladesh's National Board of Revenues (NBR) organises a weeklong Income Tax Fair alongside a National Income Tax Day, celebrated every 30 November. The fair takes place in different places across the country so that local taxpayers can visit the nearest venue. These initiatives are supported by a wide range of partners, including media, schools and colleges, civil society, associations of tax professionals, trade bodies, and government agencies and departments.

During the 2018 edition, the NBR also distributed awards at district level for the taxpayers having the highest levels and the longest time paying taxes.

At the fair, taxpayers can obtain exclusive tax-help services provided by income tax officials free of charge; these include explaining tax returns, as well as providing assistance in filing tax returns and in the computation of tax liabilities.

Taxpayers can also obtain tax information, such as forms and brochures provided at the fair. As of 2018, the NBR included new features such as tax training through audio-visuals. New taxpayers can also collect e-TINs (electronic tax identification numbers) on the spot.

Impact

With a cost of approximatively BDT 150 million (USD 1.7 million) and the involvement of 3 000 employees, these initiatives helped reach 1 million people across the country.

The Income Tax Fair makes taxpayers discharge their tax liabilities in a festive mood. Tax officials, taxpayers, media and participants from civil society flock together to enjoy tax events with a happy, smiling face. Taxpayers simply love this.

Bazlul Kabir Bhuiyan, Commissioner of Taxes, NBR, Bangladesh

Source: OECD Survey on Taxpayer Education Initiatives.

Participating in other events to meet taxpayers

Many annual non-tax-oriented events are organised across countries. Some are very suitable for participation of tax administrations, for instance those organised nationwide and supported by high-level government officials. Each country has its own priority festival of the year, which is usually a good opportunity for tax administrations to participate. For instance, the tax administration of Burkina Faso participates in several events throughout the year (Box 4.7). Tax administrations can also set up stands in cultural events organised across the country to spread the word and diffuse information to taxpayers.

Box 4.7. Burkina Faso: Participating in annual events

In Burkina Faso, the tax administration (Direction Générale des Impôts) takes part in national and international events that provide space to carry out communication activities such as:

- the animation of stands at FESPACO (Pan-African Festival of Cinema and Television of Ouagadougou), the International Salon of Artisanship of Ouagadougou and National Culture Week;
- sponsorship of movies on tax culture at FESPACO
- participation in the Maison de l'Entreprise du Burkina Faso business fair.

Source: OECD Survey on Taxpayer Education Initiatives.

These are valuable occasions for tax administrations, as these events usually receive a high number of visitors and can provide an opportunity to demonstrate availability to the public. Box 4.8 below highlights the success of the Uruguayan tax administration in participating in a national event.

Box 4.8. Uruguay: Participating in Expo Prado

Since 2005, the Uruguayan tax administration (DGI) participates annually in Expo Prado (the International Livestock Exposition and International Agro Industrial and Commercial Exhibition), a prestigious 12-day event which has been organised every September by the Rural Association of Uruguay for more than a century.

The tax administration presents a stand at the Prado Expo for the development of an educational proposal aimed at schoolchildren to promote fiscal awareness and civic responsibility.

On average, 500 000 adults and 50 000 children visit the DGI's stand. For a population of 3.5 million inhabitants, this represents one person out of seven.

Source: OECD Survey on Taxpayer Education Initiatives.

Events and fairs also provide an opportunity to build alliances with celebrities and influential personalities to spread key messages on tax and increased compliance. The National Revenue Authority of Sierra Leone, for instance, built partnerships with famous comedians and musicians who became advocates of compliance. Some live comedy and music shows were then selected to promote compliance among the large number of young taxpayers they attract.

4.2.2. Common challenges and proposed solutions

People must be aware of the event to attend it

When tax administrations participate in an already existing event, they usually benefit from the large number of visitors it can attract; when they organise their own events, however, it can be difficult to attract people. This is not surprising as this is the case for any new event, and even though this difficulty diminishes over the years, a few solutions exist.

Solution 1 – Information campaigns

To ensure a high level of participation in tax events and festivals, an information campaign can prove useful. In fact, tax administrations can use many tools to reach this goal. The event can be mentioned in a regular tax TV broadcast, during an interview of the tax administration commissioner, or on social media. As mentioned in the previous section, mixing channels of communication produces the best results.

Solution 2 – Celebrities and influencers

As in the Nigerian case, celebrities and influencers can extend the event's reach when they advise their fans and followers to go to the event. However, they have to be carefully chosen. Their tax morality has to be of the highest standard and their public should be one that is targeted by tax administrations.

Overcoming logistical issues

Providing the adequate logistics to welcome and assist all the participants can be a challenging task for tax administrations.

Solution 1 – Outsourcing the organisation of events

Some tax administrations are considering outsourcing activities within festivals they organise. While this has not been done yet, outsourcing the organisation of events can reduce logistical issues. This may be a convenient option but may increase the cost of the event.

Solution 2 – Existing events

As highlighted previously, participating in already existing events can be a way to reduce costs, as it avoids the burden of organisation. When no existing event is deemed appropriate for the tax administration to participate, it may be possible to partner with other taxpayer education initiatives to organise events together. This is a way of sharing costs and effort, as well as pooling organisational skills and know-how.

4.3. Tailored communication

Sometimes, mass communication, events, TV shows and magazines may not suffice to reach specific groups of the population, especially in the most vulnerable or remote ones. Other times, tailoring a message to the needs and interests of a specific group of taxpayers may be necessary to ensure it is understood and accepted.

Many tax administrations adapt their communication to their audiences; some go even further by working with external experts (usually academics or researchers) to understand their audiences better. Scientific methods are used to produce useful knowledge allowing tax administrations to adapt their behaviour and helping scholars to understand better the way society works. For instance, research on the effects of different messages sent to taxpayers can help establish which communication strategies administrations should adopt while offering a unique perspective to scholars on the way people relate to a given message.

Scholars have been conducting studies on people's lives for centuries. They have accumulated an important amount of knowledge and know-how, and tax administrations can benefit from them. In return, scholars are usually interested in new fields of study and in the capacity of tax administrations to launch large-scale studies. This creates fruitful synergies for producing interesting and new knowledge.

4.3.1. Selected policy options

Communication with specific groups of taxpayers

A potentially fruitful strategy to help taxpayers and, at the same time, raise tax compliance is to target specific segments of the population and provide them with tailored information. This can consist of guidance on how to file tax returns and explanations of what taxes to declare. The target group can be any subset of the population with specific needs, such as new entrepreneurs and newly registered taxpayers. This is the approach of the Irish Revenue, which organises a communication programme for income-tax customers, newly registered cases and pay-as-you-earn (PAYE) taxpayers.

New entrepreneurs constitute a common target for tax administrations to provide guidance on tax obligations. In the case of the Finnish Tax Administration, for instance, guidance calls are made when companies are set up, explaining how and when to file and pay taxes. Portugal's Tax and Customs Authority also guides new entrepreneurs via informative emails.

Other categories of taxpayers targeted by tax administrations include auditors, property owners and foreign workers; this last group, which composes a big part, for instance, of Norway's economy, is provided with information and professional guidance by the Norwegian Tax Administration. The latter has hired two language managers so that enquiries made to the administration in English can always be addressed in English.

Tax administrations also aim at ensuring that everybody has access to tax information, especially the most vulnerable taxpayers. For instance, the Togolese Tax Administration (Office Togolais des Recettes, OTR) organises awareness campaigns to increase public compliance, with financial assistance from the African Bank of Development (Box 4.9).

Another strategy consists in organising information sessions on the official social media pages of the tax administration, as done by Romania's National Agency for Fiscal Administration (NAFA). NAFA embarked on this initiative after a survey that made it clear that not every taxpayer uses service channels like websites for submitting a tax return or reading a guideline. Thanks to the survey responses, NAFA also noted that reading the information in the user's preferred language, thanks to instant translation, helped in reaching taxpayers around the world and avoiding misinformation.

Box 4.9. Togo: Raising local awareness about fiscal citizenship

Within the framework of the programme called *Sensibilisation de proximité des contribuables et du grand public au civisme fiscal* (Raising local awareness among taxpayers and the general public about fiscal citizenship) the Togolese tax administration (OTR) organises local events.

These events can take the form of meetings, attended by a variety of officials from the tax and custom administrations, and may take place at the market of a selected neighbourhood. Rather than the taxpayers going to the tax administration, the tax administration goes to the taxpayers.

The public is informed of the events by radio, television, the press and invitations. Information and awareness sessions are held interactively in local languages to facilitate understanding by all. Skits are performed to better explain the concepts to the population.

The African Development Bank provided financial assistance for several years, but the programme is now run without any financial support. It has reached more than 70 000 people.

Source: OECD Survey on Taxpayer Education Initiatives.
Image: OTR, Togo.

Using behavioural insights to nudge compliance

Behavioural insights can help enhance the impact of messages to taxpayers. There has been extensive use and evaluation of behavioural insights in the field of reminder letters to debtors. Changing the standard format of these letters, simplifying them and adding social norm messages and minority norm frames have been found to increase the reactiveness of debtors regarding payment of the amounts due, as well as the total revenue raised.

Mascagni et al. (2017[2])**ran an experiment in Rwanda in partnership with the Rwanda Revenue Authority in the framework of a project on tax compliance carried out by the African Tax Administration Forum (ATAF) and the International Centre for Tax and Development (ICTD).** The experiment tested not only the content of messages, but also the means of delivery – namely whether reminder messages sent via e-mail, post or SMS worked best. The main conclusion was that soft approaches are more effective in nudging taxpayer compliance, as compared to deterrence. Messages with fiscal exchange primes ("By paying your taxes you make it possible to educate our children, fund our healthcare, and keep us safe. Pay taxes. Build Rwanda. Be proud.") as well as gentle reminders ("Tax filing period open until 31st March 2016.") worked better than deterrence messages ("Pay your taxes on time and avoid fines and penalties.") Moreover, e-mails were found to be the most effective means of delivery, followed by letters and SMS. In total, the experiment led to an increase in compliance of 16-23.7% and to additional taxes paid amounting to RWF 6.8 billion, i.e., around USD 8.3 million.

Hallsworth et al. (2017[3]) **ran two natural field experiments in the UK.** They led to the collection of GBP 4.9 million in the first 23 days for the first experiment and GBP 9.3 million for the second. The messages they found the most effective when included in reminder letters were social norm messages, especially one on a minority norm frame ("Nine out of ten people in the UK pay their tax on time. You are currently in the very small minority of people who have not paid us yet.") The authors concluded that "there is value in adopting an approach that incorporates moral costs into taxpayer communication. These costs can be increased by presenting messages relating to social norms (both injunctive and descriptive), public services and moral duty." (Hallsworth et al., 2017, p. 26[3]). Belgium also ran similar experiments (Box 4.10).

Brockmeyer et al. (Brockmeyer et al., 2019[4])**studied a campaign in Costa Rica, where the tax administration sent non-filing firms e-mails asking them to file income tax returns.** The messages were built around relevant suggestions from the behavioural psychology field, i.e., they were personalised, simplified, featured a call to action with an immediate deadline, provided a link to the tax form and contained a social norm message ("8 out of 10 [tax-registered] Costa Ricans have filed their 2014 income tax return.") The authors found that the e-mails led to an increase of 21% in filing rates and of USD 15 in the amount paid.

These findings are extremely useful. On the one hand, they demonstrate that soft approaches based on research methods are useful in increasing compliance and that behavioural insight messages can raise the awareness of the taxpayer. On the other hand, they are also extremely cost-efficient and constitute an easy way for tax administrations to accelerate and increase payments as well as to give a positive perception of the administration. In the words of Mick Moore,

> *"These new research techniques are smart. Their use not only makes governments look intelligent, but can actually make governments more intelligent, at least when it comes to dealing with their taxpayers. It is possible for governments to collect more revenue through inducing taxpayers to be more compliant with their obligations, without in the process irritating or upsetting the taxpayers – and possibly even inducing in them a bit of empathy for the tax collectors." (Moore, 2019[5])*

The benefit of collaborating with academics is that experiments, and in this case randomised-control trials, make it easy to understand which approach is the most adapted to the target audience, and hence the one which will have the highest impact. Testing is also essential to verify whether the effects of the interventions are short-term or extend even into the longer term. Moreover, scholarly support in the project design and evaluation are invaluable elements for a tax administration.

Box 4.10. Belgium: Use of public goods messages

In a scientific project in collaboration with behavioural economics academics, the Belgian Federal Public Service Finance (FPSF) tested letters containing behavioural insights among a target group of personal income taxpayers.

The letters reminded taxpayers who had missed the filing or payment deadline to file their taxes; some of them contained public-goods messages concerning the services are provided in return for taxes.

This collaboration included a series of five experiments, run between 2014 and 2016, whose main result was the finding that simplifying the reminder messages sent to taxpayers increases tax compliance (De Neve et al., 2021[6]). Simplification implies, in this case, shorter letters with less information provided and with the action-relevant information for the taxpayer highlighted. The returns of simplified reminder letters were estimated at EUR 3.84 million, about 50 times more than the EUR 80 000 cost of the initiative (De Neve et al., 2021[6]).

Apart from increasing compliance and timely payment, FPSF's objective was to raise awareness regarding how tax money is spent and to close the perceived gap between tax payments and the resulting services. This is why the public-goods letters contained graphs showing the distribution of tax expenditures. In its answer to the OECD survey, Belgium noted that although no direct effect on tax compliance was noted in the short term, raising awareness through public-goods messages is good for tax morale and could have positive effects in the long run.

Source: OECD Survey on Taxpayer Education Initiatives.

Using ethnographic research to improve outreach methods

Ethnographic research is another scientific method that can provide vital insights into the needs of specific taxpayer audiences (see Box 4.11). It can provide in-depth information that quantitative data cannot. For instance, it can contribute to the in-depth analysis of the dynamics of the informal economy or highlight key needs of specific groups of taxpayers. In fact, it offers precious information on taxpayer behaviour and allows tax administrations not only to understand them better, but also to measure the impact of its actions and understand the reasons behind a success or a failure.

Using ethnography requires unique resources. Tax administrations need to understand how ethnographic research works, and clearly delimit what they are and are not expected to do. They must be able to explain what they want to achieve with the research and devote financial and logistical resources to the project.

Box 4.11. Canada: Ethnographic research projects

Canada's CRA is an example of a tax administration that makes use of ethnography to support its communications (OECD, 2019[7]). The CRA is using ethnographic research to better understand the experiences of client groups, with a view to improving services to taxpayers. The methods used include immersion, participant observation and semi-structured interviews to collect granular data that provide insights into people's experiences and behaviour.

The three ethnographic research projects undertaken to date have focussed on

- small businesses
- homeless people and housing-insecure individuals
- vulnerable newcomers.

The results of these projects have helped the CRA improve its outreach methods and services to these populations. For example, with a better understanding of the barriers that homeless individuals face in accessing benefits, the CRA has been able to develop outreach materials that are tailored to their needs.

Source: OECD Survey on Taxpayer Education Initiatives.

4.3.2. Common challenges and proposed solutions

Thoroughly targeting audiences

Maximising the reach of information campaigns must be a high priority for tax administrations, which must ensure that the messages sent to taxpayers do not go unnoticed. Some segments of the population require special attention, as they have had little contact with the administration. Reaching out to these groups of taxpayers with innovative campaigns is important in many countries.

Solution 1 – Direct contacts

This issue is commonly solved by getting in touch physically with taxpayers. For instance, mobile tax units are useful to make a step towards taxpayers and inform them of tax rights and duties, as will be seen in Chapter 5.2.

Solution 2 – Partnerships

Other than the tax administration's usual channels of communication – such as websites, social media and tax offices – it can be useful to rely on other entities to promote informative materials. An example is Slovenia's FARS, which worked with the Government Communication Office for the first year of a campaign on the importance of checking invoices.

Tax secrecy

Scholars may need information covered by tax secrecy to be able to carry out their studies. This is an important issue, as breaking tax secrecy can lead to prosecution.

Solution 1 – Designing studies in a way to avoid the issue of tax secrecy

To overcome this issue, scholars and tax administrations should collectively design the scope of the study. Meetings should be held well in advance to discuss the kind of information necessary for the study to generate valuable results, both for tax administrations and the research community.

Solution 2 – Collecting information by the tax administration on behalf of the researcher

Within a research protocol, scholars can prepare quantitative or qualitative tools, such as questionnaires, for the tax administration to administer. The latter can select relevant taxpayers, using data covered by tax secrecy, send them the questionnaires, collect the answers and prepare anonymised results in a way agreed with the researcher.

4.4. Impacts

Measuring impact is an important part of each initiative, as it is the only way to understand what its effects are. Are they positive? Are there unintended effects? What is their magnitude? Do taxpayers like them?

The initiatives featured in this chapter aim at producing direct short-term benefits, sometimes on a very large scale, which renders measuring impacts difficult. Only a limited number of initiatives benefited from formal evaluations. For instance, while 10 of the 27 information campaigns benefited from evaluations, only two (less than one-quarter of them) were conducted by external organisations.

Evaluations are often used to collect quantitative data, such as the number of people watching a TV broadcast or the number of leaflets distributed during an event. For instance, in the case of the Irish PAYE initiative (Box 4.12), they made it possible to measure its direct short-term impacts. However, this may not be sufficient to truly understand how successful the programme was, what other effects it may have and how it was perceived by taxpayers.

Measuring the impact of an initiative must be anticipated. The design of an initiative should include the tools to measure its success. This is an activity in itself and resources must be devoted to it.

4.4.1. A more knowledgeable and compliant population

Many of the initiatives described in this chapter have led to remarkable progress in terms of taxpayer knowledge and their willingness to engage in voluntary compliance. In the case of the initiatives implemented by Togo's OTR, the non-compliance rate was lowered; in addition, the relationship between OTR and taxpayers was consolidated, with the latter's fear towards the former being dissipated. The Norwegian Tax Administration noted, in its response to the survey, that the evaluation of their initiatives confirmed that they have achieved their main goals of information dissemination and professional guidance aimed at providing good service, informing, educating and promoting a culture of compliance.

This also has spill-over effects, as successful interaction with taxpayers can provide a prolonged and constant future link with them. As an example, the Swedish Tax Agency (STA) found that, after having provided new businesses with information on their duties in terms of how much tax to file and how to do it, 99% of participants in a survey stated that they would use the STA's education materials when starting their business.

Box 4.12. Ireland: A letter to PAYE taxpayers

Ireland's Revenue established an annual communications programme for PAYE taxpayers. Since 2016, Revenue has written letters to over 125,000 PAYE taxpayers each year to advise them of the range of tax credits and relief available, remind them of the statutory four-year time limit for claiming their entitlements and inform them of the need to advise Revenue of any additional income sources they may have. A press release was issued to publicise the letter campaign and disseminated to newspapers and radio stations.

Contact by letter was chosen because the majority of these taxpayers were not registered for Revenue's online services. The recipients of the letters were selected based on an analysis of past behaviour – in particular, letters were sent to taxpayers who had a history of paying tax in the past four years but who had not claimed any additional tax relief or credits, nor declared any additional income. The letter highlighted the benefits of using Revenue's online services to claim credits and tax relief, and outlined how to register for them.

Revenue remarked that prior to this direct contact, none of the targeted taxpayers had engaged with Revenue for over four years. While it cannot be said that all of the activity that followed the letters was directly and exclusively a result of the contact, it is reasonable to assume that most taxpayers in this group were unlikely to make a claim or declare additional income had the contact by Revenue not been made.

2016 letter

- In the six months after the letters were sent, 15% of recipients requested a review of their taxes, claimed credits, relief or exemptions, or declared additional income.
- A total of EUR 27.6m was refunded or credited to taxpayers based on these claims.
- A total of EUR 1.2m in taxes was paid on the additional income declared.
- There was a 26% increase amongst letter recipients in the number of registrations for Revenue's online services.

2017 letter

- In the six months after the letters were sent, 14.5% of recipients requested a review of their taxes, claimed credits, relief or exemptions, or declared additional income.
- A total of EUR 27.8m was refunded or credited to taxpayers based on these claims.
- A total of EUR 0.95m in taxes was paid on the additional income declared.
- There was a 19% increase amongst letter recipients in the number of registrations for Revenue's online services.

Source: OECD Survey on Taxpayer Education Initiatives.

4.4.2. Improved relationships with taxpayers through scientific methods

When tax administrations use scientific methods to improve their relationship with taxpayers, the outcome is twofold. First, it increases revenue collected as shown previously. Second, tax administrations gain profound knowledge of people living in their country and scholars benefit from this knowledge and can focus their study on well-defined groups of people.

One of the advantages of using scientific methods is that tools to measure impact are embedded in the methodology. As shown above, these studies led to significant results in terms of tax collection.

They are also a way for tax administrations to support research within the country by offering scholars new possibilities.

However, the use of these methods is recent and not enough time has yet elapsed to enable assessments of their results over the long term. This does not reduce the short-term benefit they provide but calls for longitudinal studies of their results.

4.4.3. A more positive perception of the tax administration

Conveying the right messages to taxpayers can improve their perception of the tax administration. It is important to communicate with taxpayers and provide them with all the information they need so that they fully understand their rights and obligations and comply voluntarily. Many of the initiatives in this chapter have led to positive spill-overs, not only in terms of tax compliance, and knowledge and skills, but also concerning the image taxpayers have of tax authorities (and, consequently, of the Government). For instance, by participating in different events organised in the country the tax administration of Burkina Faso discovered that some taxpayers were afraid to deal with it. These events offered the perfect occasion to change that.

Evaluating the impacts of events and fairs is a challenging task, as gathering practical information on the effects of these initiatives can be difficult. Tax administrations should thus devote more attention to conducting surveys – both to receive feedback and to track the profiles of the attendees – so that more attention can be paid to reaching groups of taxpayers that were not properly involved.

Tax administrations consider tax events to have a positive effect on tax culture and citizenship. Those that have undertaken this kind of initiative have noticed an improvement in the image of the tax administration. Celebrities also usually have a positive influence on their audience. Especially in developing countries, taxpayer days can put the focus on the utility of paying taxes, contributing to the country's development. Events and festivals organised before filing deadlines can help widen the tax base and raise more revenue. For instance, after Bangladesh's NBR conducted an internal evaluation of the fair it organises based on feedback from tax officials, taxpayers and stakeholders, as well as reports from media, it concluded that it had led to a great increase in taxpayer knowledge and a sense of moral obligation to voluntarily pay taxes.

Box 4.13 presents some statements of tax administrations that have noted an improvement in the relationship with customers after the implementation of the initiatives presented in this chapter.

Box 4.13. Informing taxpayers enhances co-operation

- *The initiative resulted in an increased perception of taxpayers that the tax administration is present and always ready to share with them any news regarding the subject of tax legislation and to remind them of their tax obligations. (Lebanon)*
- *A number of the survey results show that our communications programme is having positive results. For example, a significant number of respondents were very satisfied with the website content on completing the self-assessed income tax return. Furthermore, 63% were aware of the online help guides and videos available and 80% of them rated the videos as helpful. (Ireland)*
- *The feedback we have received has been very positive. We have noted that it is important to continue simplifying the language (by default very technical) used in the communication with the taxpayer. Our presence is greatly appreciated because it conveys more proximity, transparency and reliability. (Portugal)*
- *The initiatives led to the consolidation of the relationship between the tax administration and taxpayers. (Togo)*
- *Being on social networks is a great signal that the tax administration is making efforts to be closer to citizens. (Morocco)*

Source: OECD Survey on Taxpayer Education Initiatives.

References

Brockmeyer, A. et al. (2019), "Casting a Wider Tax Net: Experimental Evidence from Costa Rica", *American Economic Journal: Economic Policy*, Vol. 11/3, pp. 55-87, http://dx.doi.org/10.1257/POL.20160589. [4]

De Neve, J. et al. (2021), "How to improve tax compliance? Evidence from population-wide experiments in Belgium", *Journal of Political Economy*, Vol. 129/5, pp. 1425-1463, http://dx.doi.org/10.1086/713096/ASSET/IMAGES/LARGE/FG5.JPEG. [6]

Hallsworth, M. et al. (2017), "The behavioralist as tax collector: Using natural field experiments to enhance tax compliance", *Journal of Public Economics*, Vol. 148, pp. 14-31, http://dx.doi.org/10.1016/J.JPUBECO.2017.02.003. [3]

Mascagni, G., C. Nell and N. Monkam (2017), "One Size Does Not Fit All: A Field Experiment on the Drivers of Tax Compliance and Delivery Methods in Rwanda", *ICTD Working Paper*, No. 58, International Centre for Tax and Development, Brighton. [2]

Moore, M. (2019), "Intelligent Government: How Research Can Help Increase Tax Compliance", *ATAP Working Paper*, No. 9, International Centre for Tax and Development, Brighton. [5]

OECD (2019), *Tax Administration 2019: Comparative Information on OECD and other Advanced and Emerging Economies*, OECD Publishing, Paris, https://dx.doi.org/10.1787/74d162b6-en. [7]

OECD (2019), *Tax Morale: What Drives People and Businesses to Pay Tax?*, OECD Publishing, Paris, https://dx.doi.org/10.1787/f3d8ea10-en. [8]

OECD (2019), *Tax Morale: What Drives People and Businesses to Pay Tax?*, OECD Publishing, Paris, https://dx.doi.org/10.1787/f3d8ea10-en. [1]

Note

[1] It can be accessed at the following address: https://www.aquoiserventmesimpots.gouv.fr/.

5 Providing practical assistance and support to taxpayers

This chapter provides details on initiatives put in place by tax administrations to assist taxpayers with familiarising and using digital tools and services they have developed. Further, it looks at programmes meant to directly assist taxpayers who face difficulties in fulfilling their tax obligations or in receiving benefits and credits they are entitled to.

The complexity of tax systems and difficulties in understanding tax obligations may lead to unintentional errors on the part of taxpayers or, in the worst of cases, reduce the efforts they put into ensuring their tax compliance. This can lead to significant loss of revenue in aggregate, as evidenced by some tax-gap calculations (HM Revenue and Customs, 2021[1]),[1] as well as both direct and opportunity costs for taxpayers which may have implications for economic activity. It can also result in taxpayers not receiving benefits and credits they are entitled to, with serious impacts for the most vulnerable in society. Given these concerns, many tax administrations are expanding their taxpayer education initiatives to provide an increasing range of practical assistance and support.

Practical assistance can be provided by tax administrations through:

- **Developing specific tools and services for taxpayers**, such as digital assistance (e.g. chatbots), e-mail, social media and tax calculators, among other options. However, for implementation to be successful, taxpayers need to understand that these tools are available and know how to use them properly, bearing in mind that some taxpayers will be digitally disadvantaged.
- **Offering direct assistance to taxpayers**, for example from tax officials or trained individuals who provide one-to-one support (e.g. tax clinics).

This chapter looks at both of these areas, with a particular focus on how tax administrations assist taxpayers in using new digital tools and services, and how they provide direct assistance to those that may face difficulties in fulfilling their tax obligations or receiving benefits and credits.

Further details on 30 of the initiatives analysed to inform this chapter can be found in Annex A.

5.1. Assistance in the use of digital tools and services

5.1.1. Assisting taxpayers in using digital new tools and services

Technological advancements have led many tax administrations to introduce new digital tools and services over recent years. This is well illustrated by the country examples included in the 2021 edition of the OECD Tax Administration Series (TAS) (OECD, forthcoming[2]) as well as earlier editions of the same series. The new tools and services are not only introduced to improve the efficiency and effectiveness of the administration and collection of taxes and other revenue, but also:

- ***To respond to taxpayer expectations regarding communication and service channels***. Data from the 2021 edition of the TAS shows that taxpayer uptake of digital contact channels (online, email and digital assistance) is increasing, while usage of traditional channels (telephone, in-person and paper) continues to decrease (Table 5.1 below).

Table 5.1. Service demand by channel

Channel type	No. of jurisdictions providing data	2018	2019	Change
Online via taxpayer account	31	943 968 722	1 140 362 160	+20.8%
Telephone call	54	339 045 062	327 330 943	-3.5%
In-person	35	109 579 208	109 041 549	-0.5%
Mail / post	21	50 372 394	49 137 284	-2.5%
E-mail	30	12 568 291	13 959 880	+11.1%
Digital assistance	29	10 942 071	21 783 351	+99.1%

Source: OECD (2021), *Tax Administration 2021: Comparative Information on OECD and other Advanced and Emerging Economies*, https://doi.org/10.1787/74d162b6-en, Table 5.1.

- ***To support self-service and provide 24/7 access to information***. The 2019 edition of the TAS includes information on a number of e-services and tools offered by tax administrations to provide self-service options to taxpayers. The data in that report shows that by 2017, a large majority of administrations provided tools and calculators on their websites as well as online services and digital mailboxes; a small number had already introduced chatbots. The information from the 2019 TAS is shown in Table 5.2 and Table 5.3.

  While the 2021 edition of the TAS does not look in detail at the e-services provided by tax administrations, it does contain new information as regards chatbots. It shows that the number of administrations using chatbots to help respond to taxpayer enquiries and support self-service has increased significantly between 2017 and 2019, with close to 50% of administrations reporting the use of such technology in 2019 (OECD, forthcoming[2]).[2]

Table 5.2. Provision of e-services and tools to support self-service, 2017

Percent of administrations

	Chatbots	Artificial intelligence	Information on website	Tools and calculators on website	Online services
Already in place	17.2	8.6	100.0	98.3	91.4
Implementing	12.1	13.8			
Planning to use	39.7	51.7			

Source: OECD (2019), *Tax Administration 2019: Comparative Information on OECD and other Advanced and Emerging Economies*, https://doi.org/10.1787/74d162b6-en, Table 1.5.

Table 5.3. Services provided via mobile applications, 2017

No. of jurisdictions providing mobile applications	Types of services provided (as percent of jurisdictions that provide mobile applications)				
	Access to information and guidance materials	Access to taxpayer account information	Access to enquiry services	Mobile payment of taxes	Reporting of a tax offense
32	81.3	62.5	50.0	46.9	21.9

Source: OECD (2019), *Tax Administration 2019: Comparative Information on OECD and other Advanced and Emerging Economies*, https://doi.org/10.1787/74d162b6-en, Table 1.6.

- ***To reduce taxpayer burdens when complying with their tax obligations***. Tax administrations are concerned about the administrative burdens taxpayers face in complying with their tax obligations. For many, the issue of reducing the compliance burden has become a high priority (Figure 5.1) and they are increasingly taking proactive and innovative approaches to minimise compliance burdens. (The OECD Forum on Tax Administration has also published a maturity model on the measurement and management of the compliance burden aimed at helping administrations to evaluate their level of maturity and possible reform options (OECD, 2019[3]).)

Figure 5.1. Relative priorities of key aspects of tax administrations' service and assistance strategy

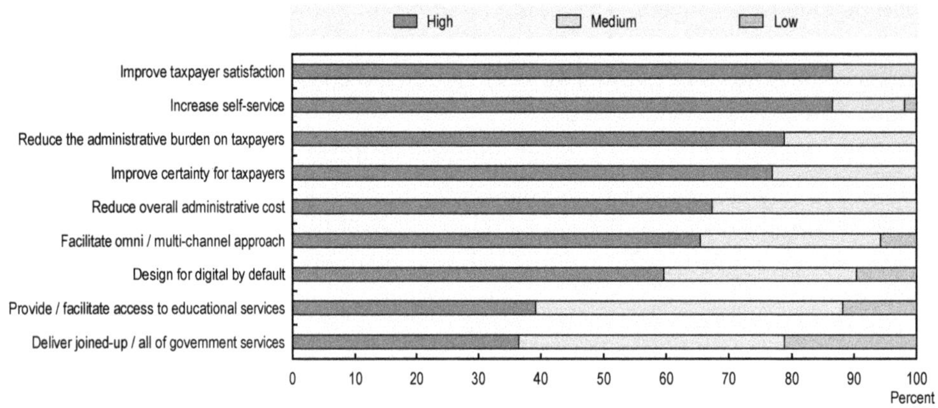

Source: OECD (2019), *Tax Administration 2019: Comparative Information on OECD and other Advanced and Emerging Economies*, https://doi.org/10.1787/74d162b6-en, Figure 1.3.

StatLink https://stat.link/uklny0

Materialising these aims and objectives requires widely adoption by taxpayers of the new digital tools and services. This means that tax administrations not only need to advertise the availability of the new tools and services (something that is covered in Chapter 4) but also to teach and show taxpayers how to use them for their own benefit. This includes convincing those who may be scared or have negative sentiments towards using technology to comply with their tax obligations. Any difficulty in applying the new tools and services (even if merely perceived) may result in taxpayer refusal to use them, which could lead in turn to reduced compliance and additional costs for the administration to keep legacy tools and services up and running.

Against this background, tax administrations may wish to consider ensuring that taxpayers are involved in the design and testing of new services (taxpayer-centric design) as well as providing taxpayers with practical assistance and user guidance when new digital tools and services are launched. This may include preparing tutorials explaining step-by-step how new tools are used or providing documents that set out the benefits of switching to the new services, including time and/or cost savings. The following section provides an overview of how some administrations have accompanied taxpayers in the use of new digital tools and services.

5.1.2. Illustrating the benefits of new tools and services and how to use them

> *It's important to find correct tone, language and media to communicate to different audiences. Moreover, it's fundamental to help taxpayers with e-service using new media (imagines, video, social).*
>
> Sergio Mazzei, Head of Press and Communication Office, Italian Revenue Agency, Italy

To increase uptake in the use of new digital tools and services, it is important to illustrate to the taxpayer population why they should use them (for example burden reduction and quicker access to information) and how to use them. Practical assistance should be considered an important step in a smooth transition from traditional contact channels to digital contact channels. There are many ways for tax administrations to illustrate the advantages of new tools and services; below is a selection of those reported by administrations that participated in the survey underlying this report:

- ***Producing videos*** and making them available, for example via YouTube or on the tax administration website, appears to be a common way of explaining in detail how to use new tools and services. The Belgian tax administration has, for example, uploaded tutorial videos on YouTube explaining how to use the new online payment application and has promoted them via social media. The tutorial videos targeted about 2 million taxpayers and resulted in a 332% increase of electronic payments within the first two months after launching (compared to the same period in the previous year).

  Videos have the advantage of being available 24/7; they can be shared easily among the taxpayer population; and, if they are reasonably short, they can be watched on the go providing tailored information for particular situations. However, one important disadvantage of videos is that they do not reach taxpayers that do not (or not always) have online access. Explanatory videos on specific aspects of tax compliance (for example filing deadlines or new tax requirements) could be shown on television to reach a wider segment of the population.
- ***Producing and targeting written communication***. Tax administrations will often know which taxpayer segment will be concerned by a new tool or service and, typically, how to contact those taxpayers (for example because the administration has the postal or the e-mail address). Leaflets or manuals that explain how to use new tools or services can therefore be very effective when trying to reach out to a wide group of taxpayers, whether by post, e-mail or through third parties (such as libraries, citizens advice centres, local authorities etc.) For example, when the Finnish Tax Administration launched the new electronic taxpayer portal (see Box 5.1.) it provided all Finnish households with a leaflet. Limitations in the tax register may be addressed by working with other government agencies (for example, those in charge of the population register).
- ***Building demo versions*** of new tools and services that can be used by the taxpayer population may be an effective way to illustrate advantages, at the same time allowing taxpayers to test new tools. For example, the Georgia Revenue Service (GRS) produced a demonstration version of its taxpayers' secure web-portal. The test version allows students (and other stakeholders) to familiarise themselves with the range of services provided by the GRS (OECD, 2019, p. 37[4]).
- ***Involving other stakeholders*** to train taxpayers in using new tools and services. Many taxpayers use tax agents or tax intermediaries for their interactions with the tax administration. In some situations, a new service may require the use of a third-party tool, for example a third-party software. In these situations, it may also be advantageous for the administration to work with the software providers to assist taxpayers in using the new tools and services.

The examples included in Box 5.1 show that these approaches may be used in combination, often as part of a wider communication strategy.

Box 5.1. Country examples: Assistance in the use of digital tools and services

In **Finland**, six months before the tax administration launched the MyTax e-portal as part of a wider reform, it created a specific campaign site on its website, which briefly described the coming changes and introduced the new portal. In addition, the tax administration provided all Finnish households with a leaflet in three languages (3.2 million copies) which described the changes and introduced MyTax on the cover. Furthermore, the Finnish Tax Administration ran a short radio campaign advertising the new portal. According to follow-up surveys, the ads reached about 70% of the adult population. Finally, the administration prepared visual marketing material to promote MyTax: posters to hang in the tax offices and pictures that were used on social media.

When MyTax was released, the Finnish Tax Administration prepared YouTube videos and instruction manuals explaining how to use the new tool. In addition, the administration created an imaginary Family (Family Korhonen) with different tax profiles and issues. The family had its own website and Facebook page, where it shared questions and thoughts about MyTax and the tax reform.

Finally, the Finnish Tax Administration organised several live events for different stakeholder groups and journalists, and held several online webinars, including an open chat for questions about the reform changes and MyTax.

In **Indonesia**, the Directorate General of Taxes (DGT) has gradually switched to online services to replace manual reports and services; this includes, for example, the transition from manual tax filing to e-filing, manual tax invoices to e-invoices, manual tax payment slips to e-billing, as well as online TIN registration through e-registration and other services. To assist taxpayers in using these services, DGT makes video tutorials which are regularly updated to follow the development of services. These videos can be easily accessed by the public through DGT's YouTube channel.

In addition, vertical units at DGT also organise tax classes, choosing themes according to the needs of the work unit. Themes that are commonly raised include filling out tax returns through e-filing and using e-invoices. The choice of themes, resource persons, and tax class schedules is left to each vertical unit. Since the start of the Covid-19 pandemic, tax class activities that were previously held face to face have been shifted to online tax classes. Vertical units can publicise the tax class schedule through the administration's webpage and its social media accounts.

In **Italy**, since 2015 Italian citizens can access their pre-filled tax returns and send them online in a few steps. To promote the new service and assist taxpayers in its use, the Italian Revenue Agency:

- launched a communication and information campaign using TV and radio commercials and publishing advertisements in newspapers and magazines;
- developed a dedicated website, including a frequently asked questions (FAQ) section, guiding taxpayers through the new service; and
- prepared YouTube videos to tutor taxpayers in the use of the service.

The number of citizens using this service has increased significantly over the past years, as can be seen in Table 5.4.

Table 5.4. Italy – Evolution of pre-filled, online tax returns

Fiscal year	2015	2016	2017	2018	2019	2020
Number of pre-filled tax returns submitted online	1.4 million	2.1 million	2.4 million	2.9 million	3.3 million	3.9 million

Source: Italian Revenue Agency, 2021.

In **Singapore**, the tax administration used a chatbot in a novel way to guide taxpayers in filing their tax returns. The Inland Revenue Authority of Singapore (IRAS) implemented a filing chatbot that uses the natural language of taxpayers to walk them through their filing obligations. In partnership with the Government Technology Agency (Govtech), IRAS developed the filing chatbot to help taxi and private-hire car drivers file their income tax easily through conversational-style filing. The chatbot leverages artificial intelligence technology and natural language processing to understand user inputs and provide intuitive, humanised responses. This enables the provision of seamless, personalised digital taxpayer experiences.

The filing chatbot is the first-ever experiment with simplifying statutory tax return submission or e-filing processes through a personalised, simple-to-understand conversational-style interface with taxpayers, mirroring conversational dialogues with tax officers during the tax filing process. Among the taxpayers surveyed, 70% found chatbot filing more intuitive and spent 60% less time filing their income tax returns. The use of familiar terms also helped the less tax-savvy taxpayers understand filing requirements and reduced their need to seek assistance from IRAS officers.

For Year of Assessment 2021, IRAS has extended the filing chatbot experiment to include hawkers, benefiting approximately 10 000 taxpayers. IRAS is also building more transactional bot services and broadening its information database with a conversational approach.

On 1 January 2020, IRAS implemented the Overseas Vendor Registration (OVR) regime to levy a goods and services tax (GST) on digital services imported by non-GST-registered persons in Singapore. As part of the outreach to overseas vendors and electronic marketplaces, IRAS published a video on its website to educate businesses on the rules of the regime. The video enabled IRAS to reach out to overseas businesses that were unable to attend their seminars in Singapore. The outreach was effective in terms of the number of registrations by digital service providers.

In the **United Kingdom**, from April 2019 on value added tax (VAT) registered businesses were required to keep their business records digitally and submit their VAT returns directly from their record-keeping software, using the Making Tax Digital service.

The aims of this new requirement were to reduce both errors in tax returns and the administrative burden on businesses. As part of the process, Her Majesty's Revenue and Customs (HMRC) produced guidance and YouTube videos, and wrote to every mandated taxpayer with information on what they needed to do. Work with software developers was a key part of the introduction of the new requirement, as they not only provide the software taxpayers need to comply with the new rules, but also offer training on how to use their products, as well as raising awareness through their marketing campaigns. HMRC also worked with tax agents and accountants, who also provide training and in addition advise taxpayers on what they need to do to comply with the new rules.

Sources: OECD Survey on Taxpayer Education Initiatives, Indonesia Directorate General of Taxes, and Inland Revenue Authority of Singapore.

5.1.3. Challenges in assisting taxpayers in the use of new digital tools and services

Lack of digital culture

A large part of the taxpayer population may already be accustomed to using digital tools and services as part of their daily life. Those taxpayers may be able and willing to adopt new digital service offerings made by the tax administration. However, other taxpayers may be more difficult to reach or more digitally challenged; for them special approaches may need to be considered.

Solution 1 – Phased approaches and hands-on experience

For taxpayers who fear using digital services, the administration could consider using phased approaches whereby taxpayers are allowed to choose different contact channels for a period of time, at the same time working to convince hesitant taxpayers to use the new service through hands-on assistance. During this period, the tax administration could also apply a digital-first response strategy, i.e., using the new tools and services to reply to taxpayer inquiries. This would give taxpayers time to understand better the new tools and get accustomed to them. For example, when the Irish tax administration launched its taxpayer online portal "myAccount" in 2016, it prioritised the processing of online submissions and highlighted the benefits of faster service to the taxpayers. It also set-up myAccount promotion teams in all tax administration public offices. These teams promoted myAccount to customers as soon as they entered the office, assisting in the registration process and demonstrating the various services available within myAccount.

Solution 2 – Offer other ways to communicate

For taxpayers who are unable to use new digital tools and services, the tax administration could consider: (i) continuing existing services on an exceptional basis; (ii) offering tailored or specialised services; or (iii) working with other partners to support this taxpayer population. In the United Kingdom, for example, HMRC operates a service through which a person can call the administration on someone else's behalf if that person cannot go online. The helper and the person being helped must be in the same room and HMRC confirms their identity and verifies that the person being helped is happy with the arrangement (UK Government, 2021[5]).

Solution 3 – Overcoming the language barrier

For taxpayers who are not fluent in the official languages, the tax administration could consider offering telephone services, tools or guidance materials in languages other than the official languages in the jurisdiction. For example, the Norwegian Tax Administration (NTA) has created internal guidelines for using English and other foreign languages when communicating with taxpayers and has hired two language managers for implementing those guidelines. Basically, all verbal and written inquires directed to the NTA in English are now answered in English. Most of the written information that the NTA provides online or sends out to taxpayers is available in English. In addition, forms and general information that is essential for first-time registration in Norway is made available in languages that are selected according to taxpayers' demographic situation. Table 5.5 shows that many other administrations are already providing services and material in non-official languages.

Table 5.5. Telephone services and material provided by tax administrations in non-official languages, 2017

Number of administrations that provide the service or material

Telephone services provided in non-official languages	Type and coverage of material provided on the website in non-official languages			
	Coverage	Forms	Guidance material	Legislation
30	All material	3	5	5
	Some material	44	45	34
	None	11	8	19

Source: OECD (2019), *Tax Administration 2019: Comparative Information on OECD and other Advanced and Emerging Economies*, https://doi.org/10.1787/74d162b6-en, Annex A – Data tables, Table A.116.

5.2. Assisting taxpayers in complying with their obligations and receiving the benefits and credits they are entitled to

5.2.1. Assisting taxpayers in complying and receiving entitlements

As mentioned above, many administrations are developing digital tools and services that make tax compliance easier and reduce burdens for a significant segment of the taxpayer population, particularly those that have grown up in the digital era. At the same time, not all tax obligation issues can be addressed through the introduction of new digital tools and services. Taxpayers may have questions regarding their obligations, particularly new obligations; may be unsure about how to comply and how to file a return; or may be uncertain about the benefits and credits they may be entitled to receive. In addition, because a part of the population may feel left behind by the move to digital, it is important for tax administrations, in their role of servicing all citizens, to be aware of those that are digitally disadvantaged.

Personalised support may help in addressing these issues and several administrations indicated, for example, that they are providing free tax services for lower-income individuals and newly created businesses (OECD, 2019, p. 36[4]). For taxpayers with disabilities, the vast majority of tax administrations report having in place special provisions, as shown in Annex A, Table A.116 of the 2019 edition of the TAS (OECD, 2019[4]). When considering introducing initiatives to assist taxpayers, tax administrations need to consider who receives assistance, who provides assistance and where is it provided.

5.2.2. Who receives the assistance?

Taxpayers who may benefit the most from direct personal assistance are those that have the lowest knowledge of the tax system and related compliance procedures (filing and payment), as well as those who cannot profit from new digital tools and services. These include:

- **taxpayers who are new to the domestic tax system**, such as newly created businesses, recent immigrants (some of whom may also not be fluent in the official languages), first-time income-taxpayers, etc.;
- **taxpayers who are vulnerable,** such as taxpayers facing difficult personal circumstances, financial hardship, low income, or those digitally disadvantaged;
- **taxpayers who live in rural areas** where there is little or no access to the tax administration.

Many tax administrations have introduced specific initiatives to assist these taxpayer groups. For example, the South African Revenue Service (SARS) has mobile tax units (MTUs) through which it can reach taxpayers in rural areas where there is no organisational presence. The first MTU was launched in

2009, following which three additional MTUs were set up in 2011. The initiative became so successful that there are now 23 MTUs operating in South Africa. Internal research by SARS showed that the majority of taxpayers used MTUs to submit their returns, but a number of individuals also use the MTU service to request tax numbers and register for tax. Similarly, the Georgia Revenue Service operates mobile revenue service centres through which taxpayers can receive services in regions where there are no offices, including the high mountain regions (Georgia Revenue Service, 2019[6]) and the Rwanda Revenue Authority (RRA) launched the RRA IWACU Initiative which aims at bringing RRA Services closer to the public through means of a mobile tax unit.

Figure 5.2. SARS Mobile Tax Unit

Source: South African Revenue Service (2021).

South Africa also makes special provisions for deaf taxpayers by having selected SARS education and outreach teams trained to provide sign language tax compliance assistance. And the United States Internal Revenue Service (IRS) runs the Volunteer Income Tax Assistance (VITA) and the Tax Counseling for the Elderly (TCE) programmes, which offer free tax help to low-to-moderate-income taxpayers, senior citizens, persons with disabilities and taxpayers with limited English-language proficiency who need assistance in preparing their tax returns (United States Internal Revenue Service, 2021[7]).

Other administrations assist vulnerable taxpayers whose personal circumstances make managing their tax affairs difficult. The Australian Taxation Office (ATO), for example, introduced the Dispute Assist service, which provides vulnerable taxpayers with access to experienced ATO officers (guides) to support them through the dispute process (Box 5.2). Similarly, the Tanzania Revenue Authority introduced a Tax Consultancy Bureau, which provides assistance to taxpayers with grievances who cannot afford to pay tax advisors and also provides assistance in the use of online services. More of such bureaus will be rolled out across the country for the same purpose.

Box 5.2. Australia: Assisting vulnerable taxpayers during disputes

In **Australia**, Dispute Assist provides a holistic approach to managing disputes in the context of taxation administration. The service seeks to enhance the taxpayer experience by giving vulnerable taxpayers access to experienced ATO officers (guides) who help them through the dispute process. It has a particular focus on individuals and small businesses that do not have access to formal representation, such as tax agents or legal representatives. The ATO guides have technical tax experience and undergo an internal training course before they commence in the role. Guides do not give advice or make decisions. They are not counsellors. Their role is to: (i) connect the taxpayer with the right people to resolve the dispute as early as possible; (ii) support the taxpayer in exploring all options; (iii) ensure that all dispute resolution processes undertaken are transparent and fair; and (iv) adopt a holistic approach in resolving all matters. Dispute Assist is the first pro bono service to be offered by an Australian Government revenue or regulatory agency to its clients using its own officers. Approximately 100 officers supported 150 taxpayers in the first 12 months. The ATO also actively supports and engages with other community organisations and private sector pro bono services to assist them in meeting the needs of vulnerable taxpayers.

Source: OECD (2019), *Tax Administration 2019: Comparative Information on OECD and Other Advanced and Emerging Economies*, https://dx.doi.org/10.1787/74d162b6-en, p. 215.

Continuous taxpayer education is required to promote the use and adoption of online services, as there are always new business entrants, as well as to reinforce the use of the online system by current users.

Ms. Meris Haughton, Chief Corporate Communications Officer, Tax Administration, Jamaica

---

Micro and small businesses, particularly those that are newly created or do not have sufficient funds for expert advice, may also benefit from in-person assistance. While research suggests that the level of tax literacy of small business owners is strong on average, it does highlight that tax law changes have an adverse effect on small business owners' perception of the way the system applies to their businesses, and that outdated tax-law knowledge could result in unintentional non-compliance (Freudenberg et al., 2017[8]). Direct support to this important taxpayer segment can include assistance in the completion of tax returns and other relevant tax documents, helping familiarise business owners with tax rules as well as digital tools and services, and assisting them in resolving tax disputes. The Swedish Tax Agency, for example, conducts face-to-face seminars and workshops for owners of newly started business to help them understand their tax-related rights, responsibilities and obligations. The Inland Revenue Board of Malaysia has a dedicated tax advisory and consultation team known as Business Support Units (BSUs) for SMEs. The BSUs are located in all 39 branches nationwide and conduct briefings in small groups of 15 people; support is also available online. The approach taken by the Tax Administration Jamaica (TAJ) is described in Box 5.3.

Box 5.3. Jamaica: Return filing assistance for micro and small businesses

In **Jamaica**, TAJ runs an annual Special Taxpayer Assistance Programme (STAP) to assist micro and small businesses in completing their income tax returns, with a special focus on online filing. The initiative is carried out during the six to eight weeks preceding the March 15 income tax filing deadline. Forty FTEs serve approximately 4 000 taxpayers annually. In addition to the regular operating budget of the administration, the cost of the programme is estimated at JMD 1 000 000. STAP is offered at tax offices and advertised locations external to TAJ. The programme is customised and direct emails are sent to businesses and professional associations to promote participation. Assistance is provided via one-on-one engagement or group workshops.

Customised sessions are also accommodated through business-related associations for their members. In these cases, the associations host the sessions and TAJ provides the technical and educational support. During previous years, participating organisations included the Jamaica Business Development Corporation, the Young Entrepreneurs Association of Jamaica, the Realtors Association of Jamaica and the Jamaica Chamber of Commerce.

The annual evaluation of the programme found that with support, the targeted taxpayer segments were more likely to comply with their obligations. The initiative also allows for the identification of taxpayer education gaps. In 2021, STAP was remodelled to provide online tutorials, primarily for SMEs.

Source: OECD Survey on Taxpayer Education Initiatives.

5.2.3. Who provides the assistance?

When it comes to providers of assistance, there are two possible options: (i) tax officials of the tax administration; or (ii) non-officials. By providing assistance through their own officials, tax administrations remain in control of the type and form of assistance provided and of how things are explained to the receiving party. Furthermore, this allows tax officials to gather direct insights on system pressure points, an advantage that may help in developing new educational programmes or tools and services for taxpayers to further improve compliance and reduce burdens. The use of mobile units to visit taxpayers, as mentioned above, is one example of how tax officials can provide direct assistance.

Tax administrations can also collaborate with civil society organisations or business associations to assist taxpayers in need. While this may require providing appropriate training to the members of such organisations and associations, it has the advantage of reaching specific taxpayer groups with targeted assistance. In addition, tax administrations can partner with universities to provide tax assistance to teachers and students receiving specialised training, or with other volunteers. In any of these cases, the tax administration should consider implementing feedback mechanisms to better understand the issues taxpayers are facing.

An example of a tax administration co-operating with universities would be the Accounting and Tax Support Centres (NAF, or *Núcleos de Apoyo Contable y Fiscal*) now operating in 14 Latin American countries. In this approach, university students are trained through preparatory classes and seminars by officials of the tax administration before assisting lower-middle-income taxpayers. More information on NAFs is included in Chapter 7, Box 7.2.

Several administrations have implemented similar volunteer programmes, where individuals or organisations sign up and, following official training, guide and assist taxpayers with their obligations. For example, in the United States the IRS operates the VITA and TCE programmes where IRS-certified volunteers provide free basic income tax return preparation with electronic filing to qualified individuals (United States Internal Revenue Service, 2021[7]). In Australia, the ATO runs the Tax Help volunteer programme for low-income taxpayers (Australian Taxation Office, 2021[9]).[3] A similar programme operated by the Canada Revenue Agency is described in Box 5.4 below.

Box 5.4. Country examples: Volunteer programmes

Canada: The Community Volunteer Income Tax Program

In **Canada**, since 1971 the CRA operates a Community Volunteer Income Tax Program (CVITP), a collaboration between community organisations and the CRA. Its aim is to make sure that vulnerable individuals complete their personal income tax returns to gain access to, and continue to receive, the government credits and benefits for which they are eligible. Community organisations throughout Canada operate on a volunteer basis to host tax preparation clinics and prepare income tax and benefit returns for eligible individuals within their community with modest income and a simple tax situation. The CRA offers training to the volunteers as well as a dedicated toll-free telephone line to provide support for them throughout the year. The CVITP is promoted in three main ways:

- In person: Through the CRA's Outreach Program, organisations that serve vulnerable segments can schedule in-person visits from outreach officers who will answer tax and benefits questions and promote the CVITP. These visits are conducted year-round (not just during tax filing season) and allow the CRA to reach vulnerable segments of the population – including those in remote communities – who may be eligible for help through the CVITP.
- Digitally: Key information about the CVITP is available on the Government of Canada website (Canada.ca/taxes-help) and is promoted regularly using the CRA's social media platforms, online articles, short videos and more.[4] From the Canada.ca/taxes-help page, individuals are able to learn about the CVITP, determine whether they are eligible, and find a CVITP tax clinic in their community.
- Traditional means: The CRA uses various print products to raise awareness of the CVITP. These include banners, promotional "postcards", posters, factsheets and more. Several of these resources are available in languages other than English and French, Canada's two official languages.

Additionally, the CRA conducts proactive media outreach through its employees in the regions, engaging local media to promote the CVITP.

Togo: The peer education project

To make the relationship between the tax administration and economic operators more dynamic, in 2019 the Togolese Revenue Office (OTR) initiated a peer education project on tax citizenship. The objective of the project is knowledge sharing and awareness raising.

The process involves trained individuals (peer educators) who transfer knowledge to their peers on specific themes. Sessions can be set up in small groups or through individual contact, informally or in a more organised fashion.

Becoming a peer educator is voluntary and the educators are also economic operators. Following a selection process carried out by the different operational divisions within the OTR, the peer educators benefit from specific training that covers:

- the concept of peer education
- corporate taxation
- good communication as peer educators
- the activities of peer educators (individual interviews, group interviews, general awareness raising, references of unresolved cases to the OTR).

The activities of the peer educators are monitored by OTR officials daily through a messaging platform. Educators post photos or videos of their activities on the platform, making the exchange of experiences instant and national. Peer educators can also use the platform to ask questions of OTR officials and their answers benefit the whole group.

In the first year, 273 peers were trained through this initiative. The project is now expected to expand digitally and geographically.

Source: OECD Survey on Taxpayer Education Initiatives.

5.2.4. Where assistance is provided

There are several possible venues for providing assistance: in the tax administration's offices, at the taxpayer's home or business premises, in partner institutions such as schools and universities, or at other government offices. From a taxpayer perspective, direct visits at home or at the business premises may be the most comfortable and probably preferable, particularly for those whose personal circumstances make it difficult to visit tax offices or those that live in rural areas with no access to tax offices. This also allows officials to demonstrate new digital services and explain their application to taxpayers while they use their own personal devices, something which may help taxpayers to become more independent and to comply with their tax obligations in the future. While more costly for the administration, in-person visits may have a positive impact on taxpayer satisfaction and, thus, on the general view of the tax administration. To make it easier for taxpayers to access support, some administrations also provide assistance in public areas. For example, in Indonesia the tax administration has opened Tax Corners in public activity areas such as shopping centres and banks.

Box 5.5 describes how the CRA expands its services for small businesses by offering in-person visits from a tax official.

Box 5.5. Canada: Visits to small businesses

In **Canada**, the Canada Revenue Agency (CRA) continues its transformation toward a culture of service to ensure that the CRA is fairer, more helpful, and client-focussed.

One example is the CRA's Liaison Officer (LO) service.[5] This service is designed to help small businesses and self-employed individuals by providing free, personalised support, including information and guidance about tax obligations and responsibilities. The objective is to reduce the compliance burden by making it easier for the individuals to comply, thereby avoiding costly intervention in the future. The LO service has been successful in supporting this population in their interactions with the CRA, promoting and ensuring voluntary compliance from the start. Since the launch of the programme in 2014, more than 57 000 small businesses and self-employed individuals have benefited from this service.

Traditionally, the LO service was offered through in-person, one-on-one visits and group seminars at a time and place that was convenient for the client. Now, the CRA is taking an innovative approach to the new work environment by offering the LO service virtually through telephone and secure videoconference platforms. This approach aims to remove geographical barriers; increase flexibility, accessibility and convenience; and provide better service while ensuring that clients' safety and privacy are respected. The service is voluntary and is readily available by request from any small business or self-employed individual in Canada.

Source: OECD (2021), *Tax Administration 2021: Comparative Information on OECD and Other Advanced and Emerging Economies*, https://doi.org/10.1787/cef472b9-en, p. 92.

Direct assistance from tax officials does not necessarily require that the officials go to the taxpayer. The tax administration can also provide remote assistance, for example via phone calls. In this respect, an interesting example is the approach taken by Canada where the administration uses data at hand to identify individuals who may be eligible for benefits or who are at risk of having benefits cut off, contacting them via the postal service and telephone (Box 5.6).

Box 5.6. Canada: Contacting taxpayers eligible for benefits

In **Canada**, the CRA uses business intelligence and data analytics to identify and send letters to those who typically do not file income tax returns and may be eligible for benefits. As a result of letter mail-outs in 2017, a total of 37 934 returns were filed resulting in over CAD 6.98 million in tax refund payments and CAD 32.4 million in credits or benefits paid. The CRA has also launched a Call Me First initiative, in which the CRA proactively calls individuals at risk of having benefits cut off because the CRA lacks relevant information. While still in its early stages, the CRA has so far reached out to approximately 8 000 benefit recipients. Feedback indicates that benefit recipients appreciate receiving personalised assistance and being provided with additional time to respond, if needed.

Source: OECD (2019), *Tax Administration 2019: Comparative Information on OECD and Other Advanced and Emerging Economies*, https://dx.doi.org/10.1787/74d162b6-en, p. 68.

Assistance can also be provided through partner institutions, such as universities, schools or organisations that operate tax clinics. Tax clinics may operate on a walk-in basis but may also provide remote services, such as via telephone. They can provide a broad number of tax-related services, including assistance in return filing and with tax disputes. Individuals providing assistance in tax clinics must be properly educated on tax matters. Many tax administrations and governments support national tax clinic programmes via direct funding, and training and certification of individuals. For example, in Australia, the government funds a National Tax Clinic programme which is available to eligible individuals, small businesses, not-for-profit organisations and charities. While the programme is run by universities, the tax administration supports it (Australian Taxation Office, 2021[10]).

5.2.5. Challenges in assisting taxpayers with compliance and entitlements

Availability of resources

A key challenge in providing direct assistance to taxpayers is that of resources. Unless the tax administration operates its own programme with dedicated tax officials, it may be difficult to find officials who are willing to assist taxpayers in fulfilling their tax obligations outside working hours.

Solution 1 - Partnerships

This issue can be addressed to some extent by working with and supporting volunteer groups or by partnering with associations, schools and universities. These partners may be of great help, and they sometimes already are in contact with the group of taxpayers needing help. The NAF initiatives, the IRS' VITA/TCE programmes and the Australian National Tax Clinic programme, all mentioned above, are examples where tax administrations support or partner with volunteers or universities to assist taxpayers. Another example is the approach taken by the Chilean tax administration (Box 5.7).

Box 5.7. Chile: Partnering with business associations

In **Chile**, the Servicio de Impuestos Internos (SII) has adopted a strategy to promote the timely fulfilment of tax obligations with the help and support of several business associations. Through Collaboration Agreements with relevant associations, the idea is to undertake collaborative work to develop prevention strategies, training activities or direct assistance, considering the tax gaps and risks of non-compliance in each sector or segment. This initiative also enables associations to have direct communication with the SII, to request specific training and support, to seek answers to common taxation problems, to help in the detection of non-compliance, and to propose collaborative solutions. The first Collaboration Agreement was signed in January 2017; 31 agreements are now in force with more than 180 joint activities undertaken.

Source: OECD (2019), *Tax Administration 2019: Comparative Information on OECD and Other Advanced and Emerging Economies*, https://dx.doi.org/10.1787/74d162b6-en, p. 36.

Providing training

Working with non-tax officials raises, however, another important issue: providing tax training to volunteers and other individuals involved in providing assistance in more complex cases. This is key for ensuring that the advice given adheres to the law and applicable guidelines.

Solution 1 – Providing training courses and certification programmes

To ensure that volunteers or other helpers are properly trained and educated on tax issues as well as the services and tools offered, tax administrations may consider providing training courses and certification programmes. Volunteers participating in such programmes will not only help other people and learn a lot, but they will also gain skills that they will be able to certify in the future thanks to the certificate they have received. This is an efficient way to ensure volunteers have the proper knowledge and skills and to motivate them to get involved. For example, as mentioned above in Australia, Tax Help volunteers guide and encourage citizens to prepare and file their own tax returns. To ensure that these volunteers have the required knowledge, the ATO trains them in the necessary tools and services, such as the online tax portal (Australian Taxation Office, 2021[9]).

Similarly, volunteers in the IRS' VITA/TCE programmes, who provide free tax return preparation for eligible taxpayers, must follow a training course and pass the certification test (United States Internal Revenue Service, 2021[7]).

Promoting the availability of assistance programmes

Finally, tax administrations need to consider how to promote the availability of assistance programmes. Obtaining taxpayers' attention and ensuring their participation in assistance programmes is important for the success of these initiatives, taxpayer satisfaction and the overall tax compliance environment.

Solution 1 – Promoting the initiatives

In this respect, it may be helpful to involve other government bodies in promoting initiatives. For example, the Chilean tax administration works with municipalities to directly contact businesses and refer them to the assistance initiatives. In Australia, the Tax Help centres are located in a range of community venues, such as libraries, community centres, and multicultural and other community organisations (Australian Taxation Office, 2021[9]).

References

Australian Taxation Office (2021), *Become a Tax Help volunteer or open a Tax Help centre*, http://www.ato.gov.au/Individuals/Your-tax-return/Help-and-support-to-lodge-your-tax-return/Become-a-Tax-Help-volunteer-or-open-a-centre/ (accessed on 20 July 2021). [9]

Australian Taxation Office (2021), "National Tax Clinic program", https://www.ato.gov.au/General/Gen/National-Tax-Clinic-program/ (accessed on 21 September 2021). [10]

Freudenberg, B. et al. (2017), "Tax Literacy of Australian Small Businesses", Vol. 18/2, pp. 21-61, https://ssrn.com/abstract=3090125. [8]

Georgia Revenue Service (2019), *2018 Annual Report of the Revenue Service of the Ministry of Finance of Georgia*, http://www.rs.ge/RsGe.Module/GetDoc/Get_File?doc_id=10602 (accessed on 20 July 2021). [6]

HM Revenue and Customs (2021), *Measuring tax gaps 2021 edition - tax gap estimates for 2019 to 2020.* [1]

OECD (2019), *Tax Administration 2019: Comparative Information on OECD and other Advanced and Emerging Economies*, OECD Publishing, Paris, https://dx.doi.org/10.1787/74d162b6-en. [4]

OECD (2019), *Tax Compliance Burden Maturity Model*, http://www.oecd.org/tax/forum-on-tax-administration/publications-and-products/tax-compliance-burden-maturity-model.htm. [3]

OECD (forthcoming), *Tax Administration 2021: Comparative Information on OECD and other Advanced and Emerging Economies*, OECD Publishing, Paris. [2]

UK Government (2021), *Help frieds or family with their tax*, https://www.gov.uk/help-friends-family-tax (accessed on 20 July 2021). [5]

United States Internal Revenue Service (2021), *IRS Tax Volunteers*, http://www.irs.gov/individuals/irs-tax-volunteers (accessed on 20 July 2021). [7]

Notes

[1] The United Kingdom's 2021 tax-gap publication estimates that errors account for around 10% of the tax gap.

[2] Box 5.4 of TAS 2021 contains more details on chatbots put in place by eight tax administrations. Annex 5.A of the same publication contains a number of links to presentations on those virtual assistants.

[3] A video presenting the ATO's Tax Help programme is available on the Tax Help webpage: https://www.ato.gov.au/Individuals/Your-tax-return/Help-and-support-to-lodge-your-tax-return/tax-help-program/ (accessed on 21 September 2021).

[4] Examples of CVITP testimonial videos can be found here: www.youtube.com/watch?v=V91NSVevH1o and www.youtube.com/watch?v=DkwX1JHG7iQ (both videos accessed on 21 September 2021).

[5] A video explaining the CRA's Liaison Officer service can be found here: https://www.canada.ca/en/revenue-agency/programs/about-canada-revenue-agency-cra/compliance/liaison-officer-initiative-loi.html (accessed on 21 September 2021).

6 The role of non-governmental actors in taxpayer education

This chapter emphasises that taxpayer education is not the sole preserve of tax administrations, providing a brief summary of the role of non-governmental actors. It looks at the role of both civil society organisations and businesses, focussing on areas where they may be better placed than tax administrations to deliver taxpayer education initiatives.

While the survey only focussed on the role of tax administrations in taxpayer education, it is not an activity undertaken solely by them. Taxpayers do not get all their information from the administration and there are numerous actors who have the potential to play a role in taxpayer education; including the media, civil society organisations, academics, think tanks, businesses and business associations.

As the survey has shown, in many countries governments recognise the potential for non-governmental actors and are actively collaborating with them in taxpayer education initiatives. The survey featured 57 initiatives that refer to partnerships with non-governmental actors. The previous chapters have shown how these partnerships can be valuable in enabling initiatives to reach the target audiences, among whom non-governmental actors may be more trusted or have better access.

The role of non-governmental actors in taxpayer education is broad and goes beyond the scope of this report. This report is designed primarily to help understand the role tax administrations can play in taxpayer education; it is beyond the scope of this report to undertake a full mapping of the role non-governmental actors play. Consequently, it may be that the typology created in this report does not fully capture all the types of taxpayer education initiatives undertaken by non-governmental organisations.

This section does not, therefore, aim to provide a comprehensive description of the role of non-governmental actors, but merely to serve as a complement to the rest of the report and encourage further analysis of the role and function of non-governmental actors in taxpayer education. There is currently relatively limited research on the role of non-governmental actors, especially beyond civil society actors; further research could be of value, especially in understanding the impact of non-governmental actors in taxpayer education.

6.1. Civil society organisations

Many civil society organisations (CSOs) are actively engaged in taxpayer education activities, but there may be scope for them to do more. CSOs are non-governmental and generally not-for-profit entities which don't represent commercial interests; they promote, rather, the public interest. While there has not been a comprehensive study of the role of CSOs in taxpayer education, there have been a couple of studies in recent years. These studies highlighted the active engagement of a number of CSOs in taxpayer education activities, yet within the range of functions CSOs perform with relation to taxation, taxpayer education appears the least widespread. This suggests that there may be untapped potential. Box 6.1 summarises the recent research.

Box 6.1. Summary of recent surveys of CSO work on tax

Both the Overseas Development Institute (ODI) (Sharp, Sweet and Rocha Menocal, 2019[1]) and the International Budget Partnership (IBP) (Mohiuddin and de Renzio, 2020[2])have undertaken research on CSOs activities involving tax, with a particular focus on developing countries. The ODI study looked across eight countries (Brazil, El Salvador, Kenya, Nigeria, the Philippines, Uganda, the United States and Zambia), while the IBP study created a dataset of 171 CSOs across 66 countries and obtained further details on 38 of these through an online survey. Both studies created broad categories to describe the various functions that CSOs undertake with respect to tax and noted how common it is for CSOs to fulfil these functions. Table 6.1 below summarises the findings:

Table 6.1. CSO functions on tax

Functions identified by Overseas Development Institute	Level of CSO engagement	Functions identified by International Budget Partnership	% of CSOs undertaking function
Analysis of tax policy	High	Research	69
Advocacy for or against policy proposals	High	Transparency and Accountability	58
Awareness raising on tax rights and obligations	Low	Engagement and Participation	56
		Campaigning	53
		Literacy/awareness	49

Source: Author, adapted from (Sharp, Sweet and Rocha Menocal, 2019[1]) and (Mohiuddin and de Renzio, 2020[2]).

In these studies, the functions most clearly related to taxpayer education were those involving awareness raising on tax and literacy/awareness. Both studies find that these functions are the least common, although the IBP finds that nearly half of CSOs are undertaking some activities in this area and notes that the ODI survey "probably underestimated how much activity is happening in this area" (IBP, 2020). What is interesting in the case of the ODI study is not the low level of activity on awareness raising, but that CSOs are already engaged in that activity and that there was an identified need for them to do more in this regard, although funding was challenging. ODI also noted that such activity was taking place in lower-income countries, often at the sub-national level.

The IBP study dataset shows that all the CSOs undertaking literacy/awareness activities are also engaged in at least one other function, highlighting how the taxpayer education functions undertaken by CSOs are likely to be linked to other priorities (e.g., providing citizens with sufficient knowledge and understanding to participate in advocacy/campaigning or to effectively engage in holding governments to account). In addition, most CSOs working on tax are also working on the way in which governments spend their resources: 89% of those surveyed by IBP.

Both reports note a strong focus by many CSOs on international taxation issues and/or corporate tax issues; there may be less scope to develop taxpayer education initiatives in these areas, as the priority of CSOs on these issues is generally to engage the government and/or general public rather than taxpayers specifically (generally multinational enterprises).

Especially in developing countries, civil society engagement on tax is highlighted in both reports as being relatively recent and continuing to evolve, including with respect to taxpayer education. The ODI study notes that many CSOs have limited technical tax capacity at the moment. This may limit the role they can play in taxpayer education currently but suggests there may be scope for expansion as capacity increases. The ODI study concludes that there is the "potential to foster civil society collaboration with the government in increasing tax compliance, while nurturing a stronger connection between tax collection, expenditure and accountability demands." Research from Save the Children complements these findings (Wainer, 2019[3]), identifying a number of case studies of successful CSO contributions in developing countries and noting the scope for expansion. It also notes that when looking at engagement on domestic taxation issues, CSOs have been most impactful at the sub-national level, where there are closer/more direct links to service delivery, as well as to politicians and policy makers. Such sub-national activities were also found to involve greater collaboration with the authorities than national-level activities, where conflictual relationships were more likely to be observed.

Source: Author, from (Sharp, Sweet and Rocha Menocal, 2019[1]; Mohiuddin and de Renzio, 2020[2]; Wainer, 2019[3]).

Civil society organisations may have different objectives than tax administrations in engaging in taxpayer education. While the primary objective of most government-run initiatives is to improve voluntary compliance, that may not be the case for CSOs. CSO taxpayer education activities are much more likely to be related to objectives on tax policy, or to improving government accountability and providing sufficient understanding of tax matters to enable citizens to engage in tax policy discussions, or to ask the right questions on the functioning of the tax system so as to hold governments to account. While these different objectives among tax administrations and CSOs may produce an overlap in terms of the type of taxpayer education activities needed, creating the opportunity for partnerships, as demonstrated by the range of partnerships described in our survey, this will not always be the case.

Equipping citizens with the tools to hold the government to account for the tax system is an important part of the social contract, and CSOs are especially well placed to fulfil this role. While the advocacy that many CSOs engage in may be beyond the remit of taxpayer education, helping citizens to know how to engage in their own advocacy towards the government, and how to use data to hold the government to account, is an important function that can help build trust in the tax system in the long term. The Uganda-based CSO SEATINI (The Southern and Eastern Africa Trade Information and Negotiations Institute) demonstrates this approach with their A Day in the Life of a Ugandan Tax Payer, which seeks to identify all the ways in which a Ugandan citizen engages with the tax system on a given day, encouraging people to reflect on the services provided in return (Figure 6.1). CSOs are well placed for this role because of their independence from the government, their generally good understanding of the communities they represent and their ability, as a result, to tailor initiatives to people's needs. CSOs can therefore make effective partners for taxpayer education initiatives that are seeking to increase the accountability of the tax system (as covered in Chapter 4), though in such cases it is especially important to ensure the CSO is able to retain its independence, otherwise trust can be lowered rather than increased.

Figure 6.1. Extract from a Day in the Life of a Ugandan Taxpayer

Note: This is an extract from 'A Day in the Life of a Ugandan taxpayer (FY 2019/20), produced by SEATINI; the full pamphlet covers the full day, outlining how each of the totals in the summary is calculated.
Source: https://seatiniuganda.org/wp-content/uploads/2020/06/Day-in-the-Life-of-a-Tax-Payer.pdf

CSOs looking to hold governments to account will often consider the whole fiscal system, looking at spending decisions as well as revenue-raising policies and administration. This is a much wider remit than revenue authorities may feel comfortable developing themselves, and it may be challenging to set up the cross-government work to enable government-run initiatives to cover the same breadth of issues that CSOs can cover. CSOs can play a vital role in these areas. In some cases, this can be in partnership with the government, in others independently. The Child Rights Networks in Kenya, supported by Save the Children, are an example of how CSOs can encourage accountability (Box 6.2).

Box 6.2. Child Rights Networks taxpayer education in Kenya

Save the Children has been supporting domestic resource mobilisation in Bungoma and Wajir in Kenya since 2018. It facilitates networks of civil society groups that deliver health and other social services to children and families through Child Rights Networks (CRNs). The CRNs work with communities to mobilize input into budget and tax processes.

The activities undertaken by the CRNs include radio programmes and flyers to inform citizens about tax, highlighting the importance of everyone contributing their fair share and illustrating how to participate in tax policy processes.

In Bungoma, CRNs have helped citizens to analyse the operation of the existing tax laws for business permits and market fees, leading to reform proposals being provided to the local county assembly, and adopted. These reforms appear to have been successful, in part thanks to the engagement of taxpayers in the reforms, encouraging compliance because of the taxpayers' perceived ownership of the policy.

The initiative has also improved the relationship between the CRNs and the government. The relationship had previously been conflictual, as the CRNs had only been advocating on spending decisions, with no recognition of the challenges of restricted budgets. With CRNs now taking a broader focus on tax and spending together, the relationship is reported to have improved, with a greater sense of shared purpose between CSOs and government. This highlights how increasing taxpayer education to hold governments to account does not need to be adversarial.

Source: Save the Children.

Civil society organisations may have more diverse resources, flexibility and access to creative skills, which can help in creating engaging taxpayer education initiatives. While the previous chapters of this report have shown that many governments have been innovative and creative in their approaches to taxpayer education, it can be hard to encourage such an approach within government structures. As reported by many in the survey, securing sufficient resources, both human and financial, is a constraint on many government-run initiatives; in addition, bureaucratic procedures can stifle the creativity of initiatives. While CSOs also struggle with resources, especially financial, the CSOs undertaking taxpayer education initiatives may give them higher priority – and resources – and may be better able to work flexibly, drawing on creative skills for citizen engagement within the organisation.

6.2. Businesses

Businesses and business associations can play a valuable role in taxpayer education, especially for SMEs. While large businesses will generally have tax skills in-house (or be able to contract them), SMEs, especially new (or newly formalised) businesses may be more comfortable accessing information on tax compliance through peers, rather than the government. This may be especially important where the taxpayer has limited trust in and/or experience in interacting with the government and may fear that seeking assistance could result in an investigation or audit. This role has been highlighted by several governments in explaining the importance of partnerships with business associations for the delivery of some initiatives; 14 initiatives featured in the survey were in partnership with business associations.

Providing taxpayer education for companies in the supply chain appears underutilised, but with potential. In an OECD survey on tax-official perceptions of taxpayer behaviour (OECD, forthcoming) in all regions, multinational enterprises (MNEs) were perceived as being more compliant than local companies. While this may in part be a result of their greater resources, including greater access to professional tax skills and services, it does suggest that MNEs could play a useful role in building compliance with local companies in their supply chain. One company that has taken this approach is Safaricom in Kenya. Box 6.3 below shows how Safaricom's requirement that its vendors demonstrate compliance has led to Safaricom engaging in taxpayer education activities.

Box 6.3. Taxpayer education in the supply chain: Safaricom

Safaricom is Kenya's biggest corporate taxpayer and together with 19 other companies has committed to the B Team Responsible Tax Principles, which aim to raise the bar on how businesses approach tax and transparency.

As part of this commitment, Safaricom goes beyond its own operations when it comes to compliance. The company ensures tax compliance more broadly by requiring that its vendors – both existing and potential – comply with tax laws. Specifically, tax compliance verification is required before the company will engage procurement partners.

Recognising that vendors may need assistance, Safaricom does not simply make these demands of its vendors – it supports them. If the tax compliance of a vendor is in question, Safaricom partners with them to address the issue. The company also hosts forums for suppliers and partner agents, such as its mobile-money partners, to raise awareness of tax policies and promote tax compliance.

Source: Adapted from "The B Team Responsible Tax Principles in Action: Safaricom's efforts to promote tax compliance in Kenya" (https://bit.ly/2ZXxzeB).

Social enterprises can respond innovatively to specific niches. The survey of government-administered initiatives highlighted that specific groups may have specific needs for taxpayer education, and that it can be challenging for governments to effectively design initiatives to reach such groups. Governments often report partnering with non-governmental actors in such cases, but non-governmental actors may also develop their own initiatives without government involvement. Social enterprises may be especially well-suited to such activities, as social enterprises are businesses that have specific social objectives as their primary purpose; they therefore are able to combine effective business strategies with a social-benefit purpose. CabDost in India is an example of a social enterprise emerging to support the specific niche of taxi drivers, adopting a range of innovative methods and combining taxpayer education with a broader mission to enable formalisation and access to finance (see (OECD, 2019[4]) box 2.1) .

6.3. The future for non-governmental actors

Non-governmental actors can play several roles in taxpayer education, but their full potential has not yet been realised. There are good examples of both CSO and business engagement in taxpayer education, however these are relatively limited. From the limited studies/research available, it seems there is untapped (or at least unreported) potential for non-governmental actors to engage further in taxpayer education. This is likely to be the case also for non-governmental actors not addressed in this chapter (e.g., media and academics).

CSOs are likely to be vital in building a responsive and accountable tax system, but they may require support from donors and/or tax administrations to realise this role. CSOs bring skills and approaches that governments struggle to emulate, especially in reaching specific populations and encouraging accountability in the tax system. In many cases, tax administrations will find it more effective to partner with CSOs than trying to undertake those functions themselves. CSOs' limited resources in areas such as technical tax capacity can limit their ability to fulfil their potential, and therefore more support is likely to be needed by them. The ODI report encourages donors to support civil society actors parallel to building government capacity, as part of support for building a "tax ecosystem" (ODI, 2019); it also highlights the benefits of flexible funding and longer-term horizons for donor-funded projects. There would appear to be scope to increase funding for CSOs on tax, as only 0.3% of ODA for domestic resource mobilisation currently goes to CSOs.[1]

Businesses should be encouraged to share and promote best practices. Peer-to-peer learning can be very effective, and some businesses may be best placed to help educate other businesses. Among compliant businesses there should be a clear interest in spreading best practice on tax compliance to ensure fair competition, although there is clear potential for conflicts of interest if this is not well managed. Delivering the learning via business associations may help reduce such risks. Governments may consider encouraging taxpayers recognised by initiatives such as "taxpayer of the year" to become proactive in spreading best practice among their peers. Businesses, investors and others can continue to enhance voluntary principles and to include commitments to support compliance by others on the supply chain by leveraging requirements.

The role of non-governmental actors in taxpayer education should be further researched. There is limited research on the role of non-governmental actors in taxation in general, and especially in taxpayer education. As such it is difficult to get a full picture of the current situation, and especially of the challenges faced (and solutions adopted) by non-governmental actors engaging in taxpayer education. Further research is therefore needed to help build better understanding, and to help tax administrations identify how best they can engage with and support non-governmental actors in pursuing shared objectives on taxpayer education.

References

Mohiuddin, F. and P. de Renzio (2020), "Of citizens and taxes: A global scan of civil society work on taxation", *International Budget Partnership*. [2]

OECD (2019), *Tax Morale: What Drives People and Businesses to Pay Tax?*, OECD Publishing, Paris, https://dx.doi.org/10.1787/f3d8ea10-en. [4]

Sharp, S., S. Sweet and R. Rocha Menocal (2019), "Civil society engagement in tax reform", *Overseas Development Institute*. [1]

Wainer, A. (2019), "Taxation With Representation: Citizens As Drivers of Accountable Tax Policy", *Save the Children Voices From the Field Blog*. [3]

Note

[1] Average disbursements 2015-2019.

7 Conclusion: Designing taxpayer education initiatives

7.1. The importance of taxpayer education

Taxpayer education is a means to building tax culture, compliance and citizenship. It is not only about encouraging people to pay taxes, but also about explaining taxation and its place in society as a whole. Citizens, whether taxpayers or not, benefit from understanding the effects of paying or not paying taxes, both on their daily life and on that of their country. They also benefit from practical knowledge or assistance, for instance on how to actually fill their tax returns. By increasing tax literacy and tax morale, taxpayer education also results in taxpayers being more likely to help tax administrations fight tax evasion and tax fraud.

Taxpayer education is a long-term strategy whose main aim is to build a culture of voluntary compliance, an aim that cannot be achieved in the short term. While some aspects of taxpayer education may show short-term impacts, the ultimate objective is almost always to establish long-term behaviours. Taxpayer education initiatives should therefore not be seen as one-off, short-term measures, but rather as part of a continuing effort by the public authorities to positively influence taxpayers' perceptions. At its fullest, a comprehensive taxpayer education strategy should be aimed both at current taxpayers – both companies and individuals, to fill the knowledge and information gaps they may have on tax – and at future taxpayers, so as to create favourable conditions by helping them understand that tax is the basis of a cohesive society. Moreover, educational initiatives should ideally encompass the three domains analysed in this report – teaching, raising awareness and assisting – to ensure that taxpayers are educated, informed and capable of complying.

Every country has its own needs and resources, but all countries can benefit from taxpayer education initiatives. Whether tax administrations have significant resources or not, whether they have long experience in educating taxpayers or not, whether taxpayers have extensive existing tax knowledge or not, there is scope to find and implement initiatives that fit their needs. Because the population, economy, and tax system are constantly evolving, there will always be a benefit from investing in taxpayer education initiatives. They can offer alternatives to more coercive means of increasing compliance, and also bring other benefits, such as improvement in the image of the tax administration.

7.2. The diversity of taxpayer education initiatives

Taxpayer education initiatives come in many different forms. As the survey shows, there is a huge variety of initiatives. They range from teaching tax to pupils to TV broadcasts, tax fairs and webinars; but all, as outlined in Chapter 1, aim at achieving the same goal: to "transform the relationship among taxpayers, tax systems and tax administrations and to mutually benefit them and society as a whole."

Countries combine initiatives in different ways to create their taxpayer education programmes. Some adopt a variety of strategies to educate taxpayers while others appear to focus on specific approaches. Again, there is no right approach, except what matches the countries' needs. Nonetheless, all countries should consider how they can maximise the collective impact of their initiatives, establishing structures to enable information and ideas to be shared across those working on the different initiatives. The table in Annex A offers an indication of the way programmes are structured, although it is important to remember that tax administrations were only asked to report on the most significant three initiatives, even though they may, as is often the case, run many of them.

Tax administrations can also play a role in shaping a country's tax culture. This is, in part the aim of this report: to show the possible approaches existing to allow decision makers to enrich the variety of measures adopted to educate taxpayers. Adopting multiple and complementary strategies – without losing the country-specific approach – is indeed the most effective way to educate taxpayers and to make them knowledgeable and skilled on tax. In this vein, getting inspiration from comparative examples of initiatives can only help.

In this report, we have explored the options adopted by some tax administrations in their endeavour to increase taxpayers' tax literacy and their understanding of tax matters, as well as to assist them. Our study is not exhaustive by any means; it includes, nonetheless, data from 59 countries with different levels of development (Figure 2.2), different economies and a covering large geographical area in the world.

This report also takes place at a very particular moment. The questionnaires were sent and answers received before the Covid-19 pandemic, while the report is published during the pandemic. The most important effect of the pandemic has been to accelerate the movement of tax administrations online. It is not a new phenomenon, but the limiting of face-to-face opportunities have rendered it even more pressing (Box 7.1).

Box 7.1. How COVID-19 has affected taxpayer education initiatives

The COVID-19 pandemic has had, and continues to have, an enormous effect on the lives of billions of people. Many governments have taken specific measures to limit the spread of the disease, including social distancing and closure of some businesses or of entire countries. These measures have affected all sectors of society and have often been accompanied by ambitious plans to support the economy, as well as more targeted initiatives, such as Ireland's "Stay and Spend" initiative, to encourage people to spend money in the hospitality sector.

To get a better understanding of the pandemic's effects on tax administrations and on taxpayer education initiatives, in late summer 2020, we issued a questionnaire to the 59 countries that participated in the initial survey on taxpayer education. We received 19 responses, showing how tax administrations are adapting to respond to the challenges posed by the pandemic by increasing their online presence and accelerating e-administration projects, as is the case, for example, in Senegal.

Informing in time of COVID-19

In almost all countries, tax laws and regulations have been adapted to this exceptional situation. New exemptions have been granted, deadlines have been extended and procedures have been modified. At the same time, officials who previously worked in offices have sometimes been equipped with laptops to work from home, as is the case in the United States.

To enable taxpayers to deal with these challenges, tax administrations have strengthened their online presence and adapted the way they receive taxpayers, as in in Lebanon and Malaysia. Many, for instance in Australia, have created dedicated web pages to explain their response to the COVID-19 pandemic. Such pages are useful in allowing all essential information to be conveniently gathered in one place. Georgia has also inserted a banner on its website to ensure the visibility of COVID-19 related information, and China included a QR code to help viewers access the most up-to-date information. Denmark, Sweden and China have ensured an updated FAQ page on Covid-19-related questions and

Malaysia uses social media to send frequent reminders to taxpayers. The most commonly used forms are also made available in printable format, as in Hungary, to avoid making it necessary for taxpayers to visit the tax administration to acquire one.

Tax administrations have deployed all available channels to reach taxpayers. Specific publications are issued in Brazil and China, emails are intensively used in Lebanon, a COVID-19 hotline has been put in place in Denmark, while TV and newspapers are used in Japan and communication channels of other state agencies are employed in New Zealand. Phone (or virtual) meetings have proved essential in most countries where taxpayers can no longer visit the offices because of health restrictions.

Taxpayer education in times of COVID-19

Unfortunately, many countries have had to reduce or cancel face-to-face meetings at several moments during the year, moving taxpayer education initiatives to online platforms. Tax administrations offered online meetings or seminars; several tax administrations, for example in Saudi Arabia and Ireland, mentioned that once the pandemic and its restrictions are over, they will continue offering online services as they have found them effective in reaching large numbers of people.

Programmes in schools and universities have been affected in different ways depending on the level of restrictions. For example, in Japan, it has been possible to maintain some meetings on site, with strict measures to avoid infections, while in Austria and Lithuania, classrooms have become virtual.

To ensure the continuity of the NAF programme, the Colombian tax administration changed its training methodology, introducing online, live induction talks and training for NAF teams that allowed students and co-ordinators to interact with the organisers and receive assistance in resolving their concerns.

7.3. Key considerations in designing taxpayer education initiatives

Analysing 140 initiatives from 59 countries, it has been possible to identify several key considerations to help administrations looking to design and implement taxpayer education initiatives or improve existing ones. Once the type of initiative has been decided following the stepwise approach proposed in Chapter 1 – defining a goal, checking the available resources and identifying potential initiatives – careful consideration should be given to the design. This process may involve contacting tax administrations already running similar initiatives, as well as discussions within the tax administration and with relevant stakeholder and potential partners to ensure support for the future initiative. Based on the information provided in this report, there are several issues to bear in mind in the design of taxpayer initiatives which are common to all types: first, it is essential to ensure that the chosen initiative fits local needs and circumstances; and second, it is important to carefully craft every aspect of the initiative.

7.3.1. Ensuring initiatives are adapted to local needs and circumstances

There is no one initiative that fits all needs and situations, and tax administration have to adapt to the specific context of their country when designing new initiatives. They need to carefully analyse the relevant characteristics of their own society and those of any targeted groups. These characteristics can include the age of the group's members, their level of education, their access to resources, their needs, the legal framework in place, etc.

Initiatives focused on specific groups of taxpayers are frequent. This may improve their efficiency but also requires fine-tuning to take into account the characteristics of those groups. Even so, some individuals may be more responsive to some types of initiatives than others: for example, some will only require awareness campaigns while others will need the greater level of support provided by assistance initiatives; some will have very little knowledge about tax while others will understand the topic well.

This report can assist designers of taxpayer education initiatives by showing them what is done in other countries, but they should not try to import an initiative without adapting it to the realities of their country. This is essential if these initiatives are to be successful, as they must be understood and accepted by those for whom they are designed.

Consider the relationship with other initiatives

The evidence from our survey is that taxpayer education initiatives are unlikely to exist in isolation, most countries have several initiatives running. New initiatives are therefore likely to take place in an environment where other taxpayer education initiatives are already running, and others may be being planned elsewhere in the tax administration.

Avoiding duplication is of tremendous importance, as resources are scarce. A well-defined goal will help on that point but only as far as designers are actually reviewing existing initiatives and reflecting on whether existing initiatives can be expanded, or incorporate new aspects, or whether a new approach is needed.

Finding synergies between initiatives – in terms of content or of organisation – can increase efficiency. One single initiative can combine aspects from different categories to offer a rich experience to taxpayers and future taxpayers. For instance, the Núcleos de Apoyo Contable y Fiscal (NAF - see Box 7.2) imply tax administrations and university to ally to teach tax to students who will, in turn, assist low-income taxpayers.

Identify the right partners

Choosing the right partners can be crucial to the success of an initiative. There is not a predefined set of partners that must be chosen, these vary depending on the type of initiative, the targets audiences that aim to be reached, and the skills and resources needed to complement those of the tax administration. The most common types of partners that ally with tax administrations to educate taxpayers are other public institutions, like Ministries or Agencies. For instance, Ministries of Education are often essential partners for implementing an initiative involving teaching at schools or universities.

Tax administrations should not limit their search for partners within the public sector but include non-governmental actors too. Civil society organisations can be useful to reach out to specific categories of taxpayers and can support communications and visibility. Academics, as we have seen in Chapter 4, may assist in designing, leading and/or evaluating the initiative. The private sector is much more rarely involved in taxpayer education initiatives, but so long as conflicts of interest can be managed, in some cases there may be scope for effective partnerships with the private sector. In some cases, partnerships may be sought with specific individuals, high-ranked officials of the country, like Ministers, or celebrities, who may help support taxpayer education initiatives.

Ensure effective management

Most initiatives will require good co-ordination among, and management of, the range of actors involved (different services of tax administrations, partners, funders, etc.) Identifying the right initiative and designing it effectively are only the starting points. Because most initiatives are designed to run over a long time, effective ongoing management is vital.

Ensuring the resources needed are available to manage the initiatives over time is, therefore, important. Most initiatives will need to evolve in response to feedback, as the tax code is updated, or as school curriculums change. It may also be important to maintain the personal relationships among the various actors involved in an initiative. Managing a single initiative or a portfolio of them requires that someone, a person or a service, be in charge. As different tax administrations are structured in different ways, the best approach is one that is tailored to the organisational structure in the country. Several of the tax administrations responding to the survey indicated that all taxpayer education initiatives were managed centrally by a dedicated taxpayer education or communications team; such an approach can create efficiencies in management resourcing, as well as facilitating co-ordination across initiatives.

7.3.2. Managing the specific characteristics of the chosen initiative

Taxpayer education initiatives have many aspects whose relative importance may vary depending on the goal set, local needs and circumstances, and the nature of the initiative. Based on the lessons learnt from all the countries, this section aims at helping designers identify key aspects they may need to focus on.

How to Identify and reach the target audience

The risk when implementing an initiative to educate taxpayers is that of only reaching certain segments of the population – usually the ones who are already interested in tax matters. This is the case for many of the initiatives that rely on online communication – such as information on websites and social networks, webinars, etc. – but also applies to seminars and workshops that require pre-registration. These types of initiatives may not attract people who are not previously interested – and in part knowledgeable about – the issues at stake.

Many of the taxpayers who belong to the most vulnerable categories are, however, less likely to proactively seek interaction with tax administrations, and may also lack access to digital means of communication. Even if the content of a taxpayer education initiative is of the highest quality, if that initiative does not reach its target audience, its effectiveness is likely to be extremely limited.

It is, therefore, important for the administration to carefully consider how to reach out to as much of the target audience as possible, paying particular attention to those with whom they usually have less contact. Partnerships can be vital in achieving this. If done well, those reached by the initiative will not only have the opportunity to learn about tax and filing procedures, but they may also gradually change their perception of the tax administration, which is especially important when those perceptions are characterised by fear of the tax administration.

Consider the timescale, and timing, needed

While some initiatives aim at immediate effects, others seek to produce them over time. Information campaigns deployed when taxpayers are required to fill their income statement have a short implementation period and are primarily intended to produce their effects only once. They may be repeated every year, but as soon as they stop, most of their effects stop too. Such initiatives can stop and start with only short-term consequences. At the opposite end of the spectrum, teaching taxes to students has a much longer implementation period and needs to run continuously over many years to have an effect; their effect is expected to last longer, many years after students have left schools and university and ideally over their whole lifetime.

It is therefore important to identify the timescale relevant to the objective of the initiative, and to design it accordingly. The timescale will affect key aspects of the design, including the resources needed, the monitoring and evaluation processes, and the way in which the initiative is to be managed. Consideration should also be given to identifying complementarities and/or dependencies between short and long-term initiatives, for example. The impact of behavioural-economics nudge approaches may weaken with repeated use, and therefore these could be complemented by initiatives influencing longer-term behavioural change.

It is also necessary to consider the timing for the delivery of activities. In many cases, this will be fairly obvious, linked to filing deadlines. There may be other relevant considerations, however, when teaching tax to students, especially when tax is not part of the assessed curriculum. Some administrations highlighted the importance of avoiding the examination period in schools, when both teachers and students are less willing to focus on topics that will not feature in the exams.

Box 7.2. Latin America: Núcleos de Apoyo Contable y Fiscal

The first NAF – Núcleo de Apoyo Contable y Fiscal – was conceived in 2008 by the Brazilian Receita Federal (OECD/FIIAPP, 2015, p. 39[3]) and launched in 2011. From then on, the NAF initiative has spread across Latin America. Today, NAFs are operating in 14 countries.

NAFs are programmes, supported by tax administrations but run by universities, whereby students assist low-income taxpayers or small-business owners. Universities decide how the centre is organised and its formal link with tax administration is often kept minimal (for instance through a simple co-operation agreement). NAFs can comprise study groups on tax and/or accounting issues and they decide how they will actually help low-income taxpayers (Which taxpayers? What kind of support? When? etc.)

EUROsociAL, a programme funded by the European Commission that promotes social cohesion in Latin America, has been the main partner behind the success of the NAFs, promoting best practices in the area and providing material support. However, since the launch of NAFs a broad range of actors have been involved by tax administrations, including – apart from the universities, who are the key actors – municipalities and NGOs, which help to reach out across the territory and provide practical assistance; professional councils, which help in resolving concrete cases and take advantage of the opportunities to present their work; and of course government and national ministries.

Another key element that makes NAFs special is the collaboration among Latin American tax administrations, which allows them to share good practices and co-ordinate on management. Receita Federal has, moreover, provided overall co-ordination of the project since its birth.

NAFs offer the advantage of educating, informing and assisting taxpayers in one process. A preliminary phase consists in **educating** the university students who are at the forefront of the initiative through preparatory classes and seminars given by officials of the tax administration, before the students themselves become tax advisors for lower-middle-income taxpayers. Attendees at the centres can **inform** themselves, receiving updates and clarifications on taxes and methods of compliance. A special function of NAFs is to **assist** lower-middle income taxpayers in filing their returns and meeting their obligations; accounting services are provided for people who would otherwise have no access to them.

Securing resources (and ways to scale up over time)

The availability of resources, especially long-term funding, is a challenge for most taxpayer education initiatives. When designing the initiative, it is important to be realistic about what will be possible with the available resources. It may be necessary to reduce the scale and/or ambition of an initiative if sufficient resources are not available.

Some initiatives are more resource-intensive than others. Taxpayer education initiatives have different costs (in terms of the financial, logistical and human resources needed). The availability of resources may, therefore, be a factor in deciding which types of initiatives are viable, or in determining the delivery mechanism for an initiative. For example, online communications are likely to be much cheaper than running a Tax Day, with activities taking place all around the country.

Consideration should be given to how resourcing needs may change over time. Some activities are short-term (e.g., specific campaigns) and are not threatened by uncertainty over future funding; others require a long-term commitment (e.g., integrating tax into the school curriculum) and therefore call for more certainty over future funding. The fact that only one initiative from the 2015 report is no longer running suggests that even initiatives with short-term goals are likely to prove useful over a longer period; for this reason, planning should consider longer-term funding from the start. For initiatives with the potential to scale up (e.g., teaching-tax-in-schools initiatives, many of which start small with a few schools and scale up), planning for changing resourcing needs should be incorporated into the design, where possible.

Partners can often bring complementary resources. Finding the right partners can help address resourcing challenges. For instance, a regular TV broadcast may necessitate financial resources to pay the channel for the time on air, but if that specific channel is a partner this may not be the case. No partner, however, will be able to replace the need for sufficient resources to be available within the tax administration, to ensure the quality and consistency of the technical content (e.g., the quality of the messages on TV broadcasts). As such, there is a need to ensure that at least the minimum resourcing is available within the administration.

Donors should be involved more extensively in taxpayer education initiatives, as they represent a key means of reinforcing state capacities in many developing countries; this is clearly demonstrated by this report. Some donors already contribute directly or indirectly to taxpayer education. Many of them are institutional donors, such as the African Development Bank. Others are private donors: for instance the OSIWA, which supported Sierra Leone's NRA in financing tax education activities nationwide; or the Bill and Melinda Gates Foundation, which works in co-operation with the ICTD to test and evaluate experiments in tax education – among others – in Africa.

Monitoring and evaluation processes

The absence of rigorous and systematic impact evaluation of taxpayer education initiatives is recognised as a challenge in many countries (Mascagni and Santoro, 2018[2]). Our study confirmed this, showing that less than one initiative out of five is externally reviewed and only one initiative out of two is reviewed at all. It is important to assess initiatives not only to evaluate their effectiveness, but also to understand their advantages and drawbacks, to improve them and to value their contributions.

Some examples of evaluations demonstrate that it is both possible and valuable for tax administrations to engage in such an activity. The Italian Agenzia delle Entrate, for instance, used social media analytics to measure the degree of exposure, engagement, influence and perception of its online campaigns on pre-filled returns, conducted via Facebook, Twitter and YouTube. This implied considering the number of followers, re-tweets, shares, re-posts and views of the videos, as well as the number of likes and of positive, neutral, or negative comments. Surveys are another way to test the efficacy and success of taxpayer education initiatives. These are particularly effective in indicating taxpayer satisfaction concerning the initiatives and can be useful in obtaining feedback on them. Moreover, some tax administrations implement questionnaires to test the knowledge acquired by the targeted taxpayers after a seminar or class on tax matters.

Research is not only useful after, but also before implementing an initiative. Surveying taxpayers and obtaining data on the state of their tax knowledge and skills helps to highlight key risk sectors and enable concentrating efforts on them and on better understanding citizens' needs. This is well demonstrated by the case of the United States' LB&I approach (Box 7.3).

Box 7.3. Research, evaluation and taxpayer education: The approach of the United States' Large Business and International compliance campaigns

Large Business and International (LB&I) has put in place a compliance campaign process in which the organisation decides which compliance issues present risks, in terms of compliance objectives, that require a response in the form of one or multiple treatment streams. This approach makes use of IRS knowledge and deploys resources to address those issues.

The campaigns involve a thorough analysis of data to support: the identification and evaluation of the compliance issue; the deliberate consideration of potential treatment streams; decisions about the resources to be deployed; identification of training, mentoring, networking and tools needed; as well as a robust feedback mechanism to ensure all elements of a campaign are continuously improved.

The campaigns apply treatment streams to achieve the intended compliance outcomes. A treatment stream is a compliance action or combination of actions that LB&I implements to achieve the compliance goal of a campaign. The idea is to respond with a variety of treatments to maintain high compliance across the LB&I filing population.

The campaign program implements continual collection and analysis of data and feedback to enhance its ability to focus, plan and execute work, and to promote innovation and feedback-based improvement. The challenges encountered are addressed in real time based on experience, data analysis, and feedback.

Source: OECD Survey on Taxpayer Education Initiatives.

Research and impact evaluations are usually conducted either by a dedicated unit of the tax administration – as is the case of South Africa's SARS Research and Segmentation Division or the Revenue's statistics and Economic Research Branch in Ireland – or they are outsourced to external agencies. The latter can include government bodies, such as branches of the Ministry of Finance or the National Bureau for Advertising in Israel; higher education institutions, such as the ENSEA (Ecole Nationale d'Economie et de Statistiques Appliquées) in Côte d'Ivoire; or external consultants and accountants, as in Tanzania, Togo and Sweden.

Academics and researchers can be precious allies in this process. The application of powerful statistical and experimental methods offer an opportunity for tax administrations to succeed in their goals. As highlighted in Section 4.3, this has on more than one occasion proved key.

7.4. Summary

Taxpayer education initiatives can play a vital role in contributing to improved tax morale and voluntary compliance, and this contribution can be maximised by careful planning and design. The countries contributing to this report clearly value taxpayer education initiatives, and have also provided valuable insights and lessons learnt that can help others design and implement their own initiatives. Based on this data, Table 7.1 below outlines the key questions that should be asked in planning taxpayer education initiatives to ensure that key challenges are identified up front, as well as the ways in which this report can help in inspiring and refining the planning process.

Table 7.1. Key questions in planning taxpayer education initiatives

Phase	Key questions	How this report can help
Defining a clear objective	What objective/problem is being addressed?	The report shows a large variety of goals and objectives assigned to taxpayer education initiatives throughout the world, which can serve as a good source of inspiration.
	What information needs to be communicated, and how complex is it?	
	Who is the target audience?	
	Is one initiative sufficient to meet the objective?	
Checking the available resources	What are the available human resources?	The report covers initiatives requiring varying levels of resources and with differing intensities.
	What are the available financial resources?	
	What are the other available resources? (e.g., staff with experience in running such initiatives)	
	For how long can they be secured?	
Identifying potential initiatives	What category of initiatives could fulfil the objective of the initiative under design?	Taxpayer education classification can help identify interesting initiatives as well as the countries where they are running.
	Is there a sub-category particularly suitable to that aim?	
	What other tax administrations can be contacted regarding their experience with this kind of initiative?	
Designing the initiative(s)	What resources are available - over what time period?	Examples and lessons from the relevant chapters in this report and examples in Annex A can help inspire and refine the design of initiatives.
	How long does the initiative need to run?	
	Does the initiative need to run at a specific time – if so when?	
	Will the initiative benefit from being delivered in partnership – if so with whom?	
	What is the monitoring and evaluation strategy for the initiative?	
	How will the initiative reach the target audience?	
	How does the initiative relate to other taxpayer education initiatives planned/already running?	
	Is the background data needed to launch the initiative available, or is initial research needed?	

Source: Authors.

7.5. Continuing the conversation

While this report focusses on the challenges of planning and designing taxpayer education initiatives for tax administrations, there is a need for a broader, global, conversation on taxpayer education. Taxpayer education initiatives do not exist in isolation. As this report has shown, they are part of a wide range of initiatives around the world, with the potential for greater exchange of knowledge and best practices, as well as regional co-operation. They also exist within the domestic tax policy framework, as well as alongside other efforts to improve compliance. In addition, in many developing countries there are significant development co-operation projects that support domestic resource mobilisation. The full potential of taxpayer education will only be realised when it is integrated into this wider ecosystem.

The OECD will seek to facilitate and support further exchange of knowledge and best practices, encouraging others to do so as well. As part of the dissemination of this report, the OECD will seek opportunities to bring together those involved in the development and implementation of taxpayer education initiatives.

Within countries, more efforts may be needed to facilitate feedback between taxpayer education initiatives and tax policy and compliance measures. Taxpayer education initiatives are likely to struggle when the underlying policy and/or compliance measures are suboptimal. Where there are effective feedback mechanisms, both within the initiative and among the relevant policymakers, taxpayer education initiatives can play a valuable role in helping identify issues with broader policy and compliance concerns, especially any unforeseen and practical implementation challenges. Several of the initiatives profiled in this report have such feedback loops integrated into their design, but these practices can become more widespread.

Development co-operation can provide further support for taxpayer education. It is a long-standing recommendation that donor-funded tax programmes should, if possible, incorporate programmes for public information, tax education and public-private dialogue (OECD, 2013[1]). There does not appear to have been much progress, however, outside of the NAF programmes. Only three initiatives in developing countries refer to support from development partners (either bilateral or multilateral); several more highlight the role of regional tax organisations as regional development partners. This suggests there is significant scope for development partners to increase the support they provide for taxpayer education, both by increasing financial resources and by sharing expertise. Such support should not just be limited to tax administrations; as noted in Chapter 6 non-governmental actors have a clear role to play and are not yet fulfilling their potential.

References

OECD (2013), *Tax and Development: Aid Modalities for Strengthening Tax Systems*, OECD Publishing, Paris, https://dx.doi.org/10.1787/9789264177581-en. [1]

Annex A. Summary of the initiatives reviewed

Teaching tax

Table A A.1. Teaching tax to students

Title of the initiative	Country	Short summary	Partners	Evaluation	Lessons learnt	Useful links
Training for Teachers and Students	Argentina	Introducing fiscal education to the school population to help develop a more supportive and responsible society that understands taxation better.	NGOs Government ministries Revenue administrations	External	Taxation is not only a subject handled and understood by experts.	https://www.afip.gob.ar/educacionTributaria/capacitacion-docente/capacitacion-virtual.asp https://www.afip.gob.ar/educacionTributaria/capacitacion-docente/material-para-descargar.asp
Future Generation Taxpayers	Australia	Including tax and super in the school curriculum.	Schools	No		
An Emerging Online Presence	Chile	Teaching tax-related matters with two web portals: one aimed at teachers and parents, and one aimed at primary school children.	Academic institutions	No	Citizens value the fact that the tax administration is concerned with teaching taxpayers about their duties and rights. The program is long-term, so it is important to plan actions that point to its permanence.	www.sii.cl/destacados/sii_educa/
Culture of Contribution in Schools	Colombia	Building tax culture from an early age by strengthening tax education in primary and secondary schools so that children develop an appropriate fiscal competency.	Government ministries EUROsociAL	Internal		https://www.dian.gov.co/atencionciudadano/CulturaContribucion/Cultura-de-la-Contribucion/Paginas/Cultura-de-la-Contribucion-en-la-Escuela.aspx
ibute my Country, Games Room and others	Costa Rica	Teaching young children the importance of taxation with attractive and entertaining tools such as video games.	Government ministries Academic institutions	External	It is important that citizens are well informed and that the government handles spending and investment in a way that makes citizens feel the need for respecting their duty of paying taxes.	

Title of the initiative	Country	Short summary	Partners	Evaluation	Lessons learnt	Useful links
The Tax Education Diploma - Teaching Teachers to Teach Tax	El Salvador	Training accounting and business teachers, and students in mid-level education, both onsite and online.		External	The potential of this initiative is not properly weighted by the authorities and is treated as something marginal. Continuous improvement is needed, and creativity is essential in light of budget constraints.	https://www.mh.gob.sv/
Tax campus website for young people	Finland	Introducing the concepts of taxation in a positive way to 15-25 year-olds using the Taxcampus website.	NA	Internal	Setting up a new website and attracting people to it is difficult.	https://www.verokampus.fi
Teaching Materials for Pupils	Germany	Providing teaching materials that allow pupils to build basic knowledge about financial policy, the tax system and the federal budget.		Internal		https://www.bundesfinanzministerium.de/Web/DE/Service/Publikationen/Unterrichtsmaterialien/arbeitsblaetter
Educational Programs in Primary and Secondary Schools	Greece	Developing educational programs in primary and secondary schools to foster tax awareness.	Government ministries Institute for Educational Policy EU Commission (TAXEDU)	No	A challenge for the program is the co-operation with other state bodies.	https://www.aade.gr/menoy/meletes-ereynes/ekpaideytika-programmata-gia-tin-kalliergeia-forologikis-syneidisis
Civil Service SAT Works for You	Guatemala	Raising present and future taxpayers' awareness about tax and building a culture of voluntary compliance.	Government ministries	Internal	By involving people in tax and customs themes, they build a certain consciousness and level of information surrounding the topic, which they can then replicate.	https://portal.sat.gob.gt/portal/servicio-civico/
Tax Education in Schools	Israel	Enhancing and promoting the importance of taxpaying among the young generation via a smartphone application.	Government ministries	External	The program should start with younger people from lower grades and not only focus on high-school students.	https://www.gov.il/en/departments/israel_tax_authority
Tax and School	Italy	Promoting the culture of tax legality in schools to communicate the role of future taxpayers and the importance of everyone's contribution to the tax system.	Government ministries Academic institutions	Internal		https://www.agenziaentrate.gov.it/portale/Agenzia/Agenzia+comunica/Fisco_scuola/Il+progetto/
STEP-School Taxpayer	Jamaica	The STEP programme is designed to change the perception of tax and demonstrate the fun side of tax.	Junior Achievement Jamaica	Internal	There is a genuine need for the programme which	http://tinyurl.com/yymtr8qw http://tinyurl.com/y5at3fpq

Title of the initiative	Country	Short summary	Partners	Evaluation	Lessons learnt	Useful links
Education Programme			Caribbean Organisation of Tax Administrations Technology Innovation Centre Accountants Club Northern Caribbean University		complements Jamaica's thrust towards entrepreneurship and promoting civic responsibility.	
Dispatching of NTA staff as Lecturers in Schools and Universities	Japan	Sending NTA staff to schools and universities and providing supplementary text material for tax education to help taxpayers meet their tax requirements and ensure future generations properly understand the significance and role of tax.	Government ministries	Internal		
Knowledge-Enhancing Activities for Teachers	Japan	Sponsoring seminars that train social studies teachers in order to increase the number of teachers who understand the importance of tax education and can teach it.		Internal		
Tax Essay Contest	Japan	Enhancing the effectiveness of tax education and the understanding of the role of tax with essay contests in junior and high schools.	Government ministries Private organisations	Internal		
Schools Outreach Programme	Kenya	Using a school outreach programme to promote a tax culture among future taxpayers.		Internal	The programme plays a major role in sensitising students about tax matters, but it is a long-term strategy that needs to be augmented with other programmes.	https://www.youtube.com/channel/UCAurhiLNO-2Qki0yVE5PJuQ https://youtu.be/_tia0etiOVA
Competition for Pupils	Lithuania	Raising the awareness of future taxpayers with a competition on the subject of taxes.	Educational institutions	No	The essay contest increases the awareness of future taxpayers.	
Ernst and Young: Young Tax Professional	Malaysia	Encouraging the next generation of tax professionals and recognising the talent of young professionals in the field of tax by honouring them with the EY-YTPY Award.		No		https://www.ey.com/en_my/careers/ey-young-tax-professional-of-the-year
Tax Fun for Children	Malaysia	Providing a fun and educational perspective on the topic of tax with initiatives such as tax camps and role playing for children.		External	The initiative addresses the way forward in creating tax awareness amongst the public as a strategic approach in	https://www.hasil.gov.my

Title of the initiative	Country	Short summary	Partners	Evaluation	Lessons learnt	Useful links
					corporate social responsibility.	
Building a Culture of Compliance - Tax Awareness at School	Mauritius	Outlining citizens' responsibilities towards tax and covering all the taxes they must pay.	Educational and academic institutions Government ministries	No	Students are often not aware of why we must pay taxes and how the revenue collected is used. After the presentation, the importance of paying taxes is understood and relayed to elders.	https://www.mra.mu/
Inclusion of a Tax Curriculum in Schools	Mauritius	Implementing a tax curriculum for students in grades 7 and 8 to promote tax compliance among them, familiarise them with the basics of taxation and trigger the necessary tax compliance reflexes.	Institute of education	No	Students weren't aware of the importance of tax compliance and how the revenue collected was used.	
Education Programmes for Students of Primary and Secondary Schools	Mexico	Designing educational programmes for children, teenagers and young adults within the formal school system to form responsible citizens and future taxpayers so that tax compliance becomes a social habit rather than an obligation.	Government ministries	No		
Teaching Tax in Higher Education	Mexico	A large range of actions to promote the strategy of Fiscal Citizenship and Tax Culture.	Government ministries Academic institutions The National Association of Universities and Institutions of High Learning	No	There is a need to raise this initiative to the level of public policy, and to promote collective work and more generally facilitate and mediate between the authorities and the taxpayer.	http://rednaf.educacionfiscal.org/ http://www.anuies.mx/secretaria-general/sat-anuies http://www2.sat.gob.mx/sitio_internet/21_18285.html
Transforming Young People into Promoters of Tax Culture and Citizenship	Mexico	Guiding future taxpayers in the formality of voluntary tax compliance with the aim of helping them become promoters of tax culture and tax citizenship.		No		
Educating Children about Taxes	Morocco	Educating younger generations about the role of taxes through initiatives such as seminars to familiarise children with the concepts of solidarity and society.	Government ministries Educational institutions	No	Impact assessment evaluations must be conducted.	

Title of the initiative	Country	Short summary	Partners	Evaluation	Lessons learnt	Useful links
Master Strategy for Tax Education	Peru	This initiative comprises three pillars: (i) Introducing courses into the curriculum; (ii) offering virtual courses for ministry of education teachers; and (iii) promoting playful dynamics in educational institutions of the primary and secondary level.		External	There is a knowledge gap regarding the state's role and how it finances its budget.	https://cultura.sunat.gob.pe/
Volunteer Programme: Sending Tax and Customs' Culture Divisions to Schools	Peru	Strengthening tax and customs education for children and teenagers nationwide through a volunteer programme whereby specialists make speeches on the topics of tax and customs culture.	Government ministries	Internal	Need more people monitoring and managing the volunteers.	https://cultura.sunat.gob.pe/galerias-fotograficas/programa-voluntariado-sunat-2018
Fiscal Literacy for the Young	Slovenia	Promoting tax topics in elementary and secondary schools to strengthen a tax culture with an emphasis on the education and training of young people.	Government ministries EU Commission TAXEDU	Internal	Teaching young people is the best way to increase tax morality.	
Schools Program	South Africa	Educating school pupils and university students about their moral, fiscal and legal obligations as citizens, with the aim of creating responsible future taxpayers.	Institutes of education	Internal	To create responsible fiscal citizens, SARS should enhance the Schools' Program.	
Civic Tax Education Program Portal	Spain	Developing active and responsible citizenship by complementing educational work with tax subjects on a pedagogical gaming platform for students of 5th and 6th grade.	Tax Studies Institute Government ministries EU Commission TAXEDU	Internal	It is necessary to constantly update the pedagogical gaming tool in terms of content, design and level of interactivity so that it remains attractive to pupils.	https://www.agenciatributaria.es/AEAT.educacion/HomeEducacion_es_ES.html
Essay Contest – Letter to a Tax Evader	Spain	Writing a letter to a tax evader to convince them to collaborate in paying taxes. Students of primary and secondary education participate in this essay contest after the talks that take place during the Open Day at the tax administration premises.	Provincial delegations Educational institutions	Internal	It is essential to work with educational authorities, as raising the awareness of future taxpayers starts at an early age.	https://www.agenciatributaria.es/AEAT.internet/Inicio/La_Agencia_Tributaria/Educacion_Civico_Tributaria/Concurso_nacional_de_redaccion_2018/Concurso_nacional_de_redaccion_2018.shtml
Open Day and Visits	Spain	Reaching future taxpayers with open days at the tax administration premises and in schools.		No		
Inclusion of Tax Education in the Plan Ceibal	Uruguay	Incorporating tax education in the Plan Ceibal so that pupils of primary and secondary education understand the meaning as well as the importance of taxes.	Government departments	No		www.dgi.gub.uy/educa

Title of the initiative	Country	Short summary	Partners	Evaluation	Lessons learnt	Useful links
Tax-Themed Computer Games	Uruguay	Explaining the meaning and importance of taxes to children and adolescents with tax-themed computer games.	Educational institutions Government departments	No		www.dgi.gub.uy/educa
Tax Chats and Lectures	Zambia	Inculcating a taxpaying culture among young people so that they comply voluntarily as they grow up and even offer tax advice to their parents or guardians.	Educational institutions	No	The public is uninformed and unaware of its rights and obligations regarding taxes. There is a need to formalise and better structure taxpayer activities.	

Source: OECD Survey on Taxpayer Education Initiatives.

Table A A.2. Teaching tax to businesses

Title of the initiative	Country	Short summary	Partners	Evaluation	Lessons learnt	Useful links
Bookkeeping Workshops for Small Businesses	Bhutan	Organising workshops and seminars to educate and encourage small and micro-businesses to maintain basic accounting records.	Government departments	External	Taxpayer education is key to encourage voluntary self-declaration and educate taxpayers.	http://portal.drc.gov.bt/drc/
Refresher Workshops by Relevant Agencies on TDS	Bhutan	Increasing the awareness of the general public about the importance of paying tax and encouraging tax compliance.	Private companies Asian Development Bank	No	Great opportunity to interact with taxpayers and clarify their doubts on topics surrounding tax.	http://portal.drc.gov.bt/drc/
Face-to-Face Talks on the Internet	Chile	Facilitating the access of taxpayers to training provided by the Chilean income tax system.	Academic institutions Municipalities Training centres	Internal	It is important to consider the needs and expectations of the taxpayers in order to offer them the most appropriate talks.	https://www4.sii.cl/sistemacharlasui/internet/#/public
Tax Classes for Small Businesses	Korea	Offering tax classes to businesses.		Internal	Diversifying taxpayer's educational channels is the key to success.	https://kids.nts.go.kr/ https://www.youtube.com/channel/UCVTdK_EozBDQ7ICMPJdbpzQ https://blog.naver.com/ntscafe
SME Partnering Programme	Mauritius	Providing information and guidance through outreach activities to encourage citizens to comply with their	Government ministries Business associations	No		https://www.mra.mu/download/ENewsletterOct2018.pdf

Title of the initiative	Country	Short summary	Partners	Evaluation	Lessons learnt	Useful links
		tax obligations.	Private companies			
Tax Advisory Council	Rwanda	The councils meet on a quarterly basis and involve sector-based opinion leaders at Umudugudu level (neighbourhood or village level of administration), chaired by the local mayor.	Governors of provinces Mayors of districts The minister of local government strongly supports this initiative.	External		
Tax Dialogue	Rwanda	Reviewing the challenges and issues faced by the Rwanda Revenue Authority Commissioner General and the business community, in order to propose possible solutions.	Private Companies Government Departments	No	The forum allows the business community to have an open discussion with RRA high-level authorities. It is also a good opportunity for RRA management to see the business community's perspective.	
Training Sessions for Individuals and SMEs	Senegal	Training individuals and SMEs helps to promote taxpayer compliance, raise awareness on tax matters, teach the institutional and normative measures related to tax and the modalities of compliance.		External	Many taxpayers display fear of the tax administration because of their ignorance and lack of tax culture.	http://www.impotsetdomaines.gouv.sn/sites/default/files/documentations/guide_des_pme.pdf https://fr.allafrica.com/stories/201402281511.html https://www.afdb.org/fileadmin/uploads/afdb/Documents/Procurement/Project-related-Procurement/S%C3%A9n%C3%A9gal%20-%20Projet%20d%E2%80%99appui%20%C3%A0%20la%20promotion%20du%20secteur%20prive%20-%20GPN.pdf
Education for Starting Businesses	Slovakia	Educating young entrepreneurs by teaching them how to start a business, focusing on topics such as VAT, tax minimum knowledge, transfer pricing and international taxation.	Government ministries Academic institutions Research institutions	External		
Tailored Education Workshops	South Africa	Conducting tailored education workshops for small business owners and individuals, including for deaf taxpayers; SARS Education and Outreach teams are trained to provide tax-compliance assistance using sign language.	Government departments	Internal	Taxpayers want to comply; that is why SARS needs to make it possible and easy for taxpayers to do so.	https://www.sars.gov.za/

Title of the initiative	Country	Short summary	Partners	Evaluation	Lessons learnt	Useful links
Seminars	Tanzania	Seminars are conducted for various groups of taxpayers across the country, grouped in either the general category or heterogeneous groups based on the nature of their businesses or their location.	Government ministries Business associations Private companies	External	Need to increase advertising.	https://www.tra.go.tz
Stakeholder Forums	Tanzania	Engaging with taxpayers to share our views and initiatives with them while also receiving feedback and opinions on various aspects related to revenue collection.	Government ministries Associations Business groups	Internal	Taxpayers appreciate the ability to air their views.	https://www.tra.go.tz
Training of Taxpayers from SMEs and Big Enterprises	Togo	Training taxpayers from small, medium and big enterprises in current tax laws to encourage their respect for tax obligations and reduce their apprehension towards the tax administration.	Government departments Media	External	The population understands the tax message better when the language is simplified.	https://www.otr.tg/index.php/fr/
Webinars	United Kingdom	Providing information and support on a variety of technical topics that are beneficial to customers, especially those dealing with a tax task for the first time.	Government departments	Internal		https://www.gov.uk/government/collections/hmrc-webinars-email-alerts-and-videos#businesses-and-individuals

Source: OECD Survey on Taxpayer Education Initiatives.

Table A A.3. Teaching tax to individuals

Title of the initiative	Country	Short summary	Partners	Evaluation	Lessons learnt	Useful links
Fiscal Assistant Programmes of Internal Tax Education, Service to Citizens in Non-Conventional Care Spaces	Argentina	Implementing fiscal assistant programmes as part of tax education events; offering preventive education and advice to citizens on a temporary basis.		No	It is important to work in networks.	https://www.afip.gob.ar/educacionTributaria/programas/asistente-fiscal.asp
Community Volunteer Income Tax Program	Canada	Ensuring that vulnerable individuals complete their personal income tax returns to gain access to, and continue to receive, the government credits and benefits for which they are eligible.	Community organisations Government departments	Internal	Various segments of vulnerable populations can have substantially different needs. Partnerships with organisations that have	https://www.canada.ca/en/revenue-agency/campaigns/cvitp-taxes-volunteers.html?utm_campaign=not-applicable&utm_medium=vanity-url&utm_source=canada-ca_taxes-

Title of the initiative	Country	Short summary	Partners	Evaluation	Lessons learnt	Useful links
					similar mandates helps the CVITP access harder-to-reach groups and facilitate knowledge sharing.	volunteer https://www.canada.ca/en/revenue-agency/campaigns/free-tax-help.html?utm_campaign=not-applicable&utm_medium=vanity-url&utm_source=canada-ca_taxes-help https://www.canada.ca/en/revenue-agency/campaigns/outreach-program.html?utm_campaign=not-applicable&utm_medium=vanity-url&utm_source=canada-ca_lets-work-together
The Outreach Program	Canada	Informing Canada's most vulnerable populations about benefit and credit entitlements available to them and explaining these to them.	Governmental departments Educational institutions	Internal		https://www.canada.ca/en/revenue-agency/campaigns/outreach-program.html?utm_campaign=not-applicable&utm_medium=vanity-url&utm_source=canada-ca_cra-outreach
The Time for Taxes Calendar	Lebanon	Sending out an annual Time for Taxes calendar along with VAT declaration forms to increase taxpayers' awareness of their rights and obligations and remind them of key submission dates.		No	An increased perception by taxpayers that the tax authority is present and always ready to provide them with the necessary assistance.	http://www.finance.gov.lb/
Free Workshops focusing on Strengthening Taxpayers' Knowledge	Lithuania	Educating taxpayers regularly and strengthening their knowledge through free workshops.	Government ministries Cultural institutions	No	The initiative is very much needed, and therefore it is essential to maintain the high quality of seminars provided and to take into account the specific needs of taxpayers.	https://www.youtube.com/playlist?list=PLsasgr3iPF0EJ0oRhgFNI_sS9rcluwLfg
Meetings with Taxpayers	Romania	Educating taxpayers in the field of taxation with the aim of increasing voluntary compliance, and thereby state budget revenues.	Government departments	Internal	The initiatives must be properly advertised in order to have the desired success.	https://www.facebook.com/www.ANAF.ro/ https://static.anaf.ro/static/10/Anaf/Informatii_R/intalniri.htm

Title of the initiative	Country	Short summary	Partners	Evaluation	Lessons learnt	Useful links
Civil Society Consortium – Engagement with Civil Society Groups	Sierra Leone	Educating and disseminating tax information across the country, especially in areas difficult for the revenue authority to reach.	NGOs Community-based organisations	No	The NRA needs to partner more often with stakeholders that can help share tax knowledge and information among taxpayers to support voluntary compliance.	

Source: OECD Survey on Taxpayer Education Initiatives.

Raising awareness

Table A A.4. Raising awareness through information campaigns

Title of the initiative	Country	Short summary	Partners	Evaluation	Lessons learnt	Useful links
Aggressive Advertising of the Importance of Paying Taxes During the Tax Filing Season	Bhutan	Educating taxpayers on the importance of paying taxes and reminding them of important deadlines during the tax filing season.	Government departments	No		
Communication on New Tax Measures Contained in the Budget Law of Each Year	Burkina Faso	Communicating new tax measures contained in the tax code, adjusting certain aspects and proposing means of enlarging the tax base.		No	These new measures improve the tax base.	
Making the General Tax Code Freely Available to Taxpayers	Burkina Faso	Making the General Tax Code free and distributing it to taxpayers, administrations, DGI partners and DGI staff.	Government ministries Media	No		https://www.impots.gov.bf
Taxpayer Identification	Burundi	Encouraging informal traders to register for a taxpayer identification number, thereby bringing them into the tax		No	Local authorities must be included. Taxpayers must	https://www.obr.bi/

Title of the initiative	Country	Short summary	Partners	Evaluation	Lessons learnt	Useful links
Number Campaign in the Informal Sector		net.			be convinced of the benefit their taxes bring to the country's development.	
Tax Waiving Law	Egypt	Writing-off late payment fines.		No	Taxpayers tend to comply when they are motivated and incentivised.	
E-Tax/ E-Customs Initiative	Estonia	All of the Estonian tax administration's services are available on its e-Tax/e-Customs Internet site. Access to the e-Tax/e-Customs system is free and widely available to the public. This portal was launched in 2000 to enable secure exchanges of information between taxpayers and the tax administration.	Junior Achievement Estonia Ministry of Finance Many others	Internal		
Guides and Leaflets to Inform Taxpayers about Essential Tax Matters	Greece	Several guides are available: guide for property owners about their tax obligations and information concerning short-term leases guide to the Income Tax Return guide to Farmers' Tax Obligations guide to Starting a Business. Others are in preparation.		No	The creation of useful guides promotes co-operative compliance.	https://www.aade.gr/sites/default/files/2021-05/SHORT-TERM%20RENTAL%20BROCHURE_5.pdf https://www.aade.gr/menoy/chrestikoi-odegoi/agora-akinetoy https://www.aade.gr/menoy/hristikoi-odigoi/dilosi-forologias-eisodimatos-f-p https://www.aade.gr/menoy/hristikoi-odigoi/forologikes-ypohreoseis-agroton https://www.aade.gr/menoy/hristikoi-odigoi/enarxi-epiheirimatikis-drastiriotitas
Bi-annual DNI Information Magazine "TAX INFO"	Guinea	Informing people about the activities of the Guinean national tax directorate (DNI) with a magazine covering various topics.		No		
Information and Awareness Campaign	Guinea	Increasing mobilisation of tax through campaigns on multiple tax topics.	Media	No		
Comprehensive Communications Programme to Assist Personal Income Tax Customers	Ireland	Educating and assisting personal income tax customers in completing the self-assessed income tax return, e-filing and e-paying using the Revenue Online Service, and reminding those newly registered to file and pay.	Government Organisations	External	The requirement for broad-based and clear communications using as many channels as possible/practicable.	https://www.revenue.ie/en/self-assessment-and-self-employment/filing-your-tax-return/index.aspx https://www.ros.ie/ros-registration-web/ros-registration;jsessionid=1824430A43E7D

Title of the initiative	Country	Short summary	Partners	Evaluation	Lessons learnt	Useful links
						17115A890B181D90BC8?execution=e1s1
Campaign to Reduce the Use of Cash in Line with New Legislation	Israel	Reducing the use of cash through a campaign informing the public of the new legislation on cash transactions that prohibits its use for certain payments.		External	A well-planned multimedia campaign is very effective.	
Promoting i-Tax	Kenya	Countrywide taxpayer awareness built through media and digital advertising, training, seminars and stakeholder engagement, as well as the use of e-mails and SMS.	Partnerships with institutions, e.g., Huduma centres, banks and service centres.	Internal		
Inform Taxpayers Every Time a New Legislative Act is Passed and Reminders of Tax Obligations	Lebanon	Sending e-mails and texts to every taxpayer registered online, with updates on new legislative acts and reminders of obligations in terms of tax-return filing and payment.		No	An increased perception from taxpayers that the tax administration is present and ready to share with them any news regarding the subject of tax legislation and to remind them of their tax obligations.	http://www.finance.gov.lb/
Campaign on Cash Use	Lithuania	Informing the public of the new legislation on cash use, and a lottery aimed at reducing the use of cash, to combat the shadow economy and make residents aware of the important role they play in fair trade.		No	STI should foresee enough funds to be well prepared in disseminating information on the lottery via social media, and thus to reach out to as many taxpayers as possible.	https://www.vmi.lt/evmi/en/home
Presence of the Tax Administration on Social Networks	Morocco	Interacting with citizens daily via tax administration social network accounts that publish videos and posts explaining e-rights, duties and tax novelties in simple terms.		External	The social network accounts demonstrate to citizens that the tax administration is close to them.	www.facebook.com/daribatouna www.twitter.com/daribatouna www.instagram.com/daribatouna
Publishing of MNE Compliance Focus Document	New Zealand	Sharing our compliance focus areas with multinational enterprises and demonstrating to the wider public that we have a robust compliance programme, including our active engagement with the BEPS Action Plan.		No	The publication has shifted the perception of the public from one that assumed that our tax administration is not doing enough to ensure that	https://eur02.safelinks.protection.outlook.com/?url=https%3A%2F%2Fwww.ird.govt.nz%2Finternational-tax%2Fbusiness%2Fcompliance-focus-for-multinational-

Title of the initiative	Country	Short summary	Partners	Evaluation	Lessons learnt	Useful links
					the multinationals pay their fair share of tax.	enterprises&data=04%7C01%7CTaxandDevelopment%40oecd.org%7C17e43b7e26824ecd8c8708d944c9c247%7Cac41c7d41f61460db0f4fc925a2b471c%7C0%7C1%7C637616455628240410%7CUnknown%7CTWFpbGZsb3d8eyJWIjoiMC4wLjAwMDAiLCJQIjoiV2luMzIiLCJBTiI6Ik1haWwiLCJXVCI6Mn0%3D%7C1000&sdata=96B6v9KiJY%2FXkI2Rx86NXbyAcEQIYE7tPJ9nIxb7ekw%3D&reserved=0t
Multi-channel Information Campaign	Nigeria	Providing news updates on various taxes and key FIRS initiatives and events on TV and radio, as well as through a the "Gauge Magazine".	Business membership organisations Governmental services associations	No	Taxpayers responded positively because taxation was embedded in TV and radio programmes.	https://www.firs.gov.ng/
Marketing Campaign for Young Taxpayers	Norway	Getting young people interested in checking and revising their tax returns online; increasing their understanding and awareness of their tax situation, as well as their responsibility to submit correct information to the Norwegian Tax Administration (NTA), this campaign uses various channels of communication and includes a rap song "Money Back on the Skætt".	Private business	No		https://www.youtube.com/watch?v=opt6LzlpmRU www.skatteetaten.no/person/skatt/hjelp-til-riktig-skatt/ungdom-arbeid-og-skatt/skattemelding
Promoting Tax Citizenship	Portugal	Encouraging tax compliance, alerting citizens as to why they must pay taxes and explaining the responsibility of each citizen to build a fairer and more equitable society.	Government ministries TAXEDU associations	Internal		http://info.portaldasfinancas.gov.pt/pt/Cidadania/Paginas/default.aspx https://faturas.portaldasfinancas.gov.pt/FatSorte/home.action
Fiscal Education in Primary and Secondary Schools	Romania	An educational project in schools, for children between 6 and 14 years old, which aims to increase tax compliance among future taxpayers and their parents.	TAXEDU General Directorate of Customs Antifraud General Directorate	No	Without proper media coverage, success cannot be ensured.	https://static.anaf.ro/static/10/Anaf/AsistentaContribuabili_r/Procedura_de_mediere_2019.pdf
Media Engagement through Electronic and Social Media	Sierra Leone	Using electronic and social media to educate and disseminate tax information among taxpayers and the general public.	Media	No		

Title of the initiative	Country	Short summary	Partners	Evaluation	Lessons learnt	Useful links
Publication of Tax Education Materials and Tax Publicity	Sierra Leone	Intensifying the NRA's tax education campaign with publicity to inform taxpayers about their obligations, as well as enforcement actions for noncompliance, using publications, billboards, mobile tax clinics and workshops.	NGOs OSIWA	External		
Motivating Consumers to Check Invoices	Slovenia	Reducing the shadow economy and cracking down on invoice fraud by motivating consumers to receive an invoice, check whether it is correct and send it to the financial administration.	Government departments	Internal	The campaign has proven that it is possible to raise tax culture among citizens in a friendly, non-repressive way.	https://www.youtube.com/watch?v=yFHLAKStHPs
TV and Radio	Tanzania	Using television and radio to reach out to the general public to disseminate various topics on taxation.	Media	External		https://www.tra.go.tz
Public Campaigns on Tax Legislation	Turkey	Informing taxpayers on new tax legislation and issues.		No	Nationwide publicity campaigns, using new media instruments in particular, provide taxpayers with practical information on new tax laws and systems, and can improve compliance.	
LB&I Compliance Campaign	United States	A rich campaign composed of events, guidance, soft letters, tax forms and other publications.	Various partners, depending on the campaigns.	No	Campaign-driven treatment streams strive to both reduce compliance risks and increase voluntary compliance contribute to improved understanding of risk and how to respond to it.	

Source: OECD Survey on Taxpayer Education Initiatives.

Table A A.5. Building a positive relationship

Title of the initiative	Country	Short summary	Partners	Evaluation	Lessons learnt	Useful links
Income Tax Fair	Bangladesh	Providing one-stop services to taxpayers with information on and explanation of tax registration, return filing and tax payments	Media Educational institutions Tax associations Government departments Trade bodies	Internal	The Income Tax Fair helps taxpayers discharge their tax liabilities in a festive mood. Tax officials, taxpayers, media, and participants from civil society come together and enjoy tax events.	https://www.thedailystar.net/city/news/weeklong-income-tax-fair-begins-tuesday-1658809
National Income Tax Day	Bangladesh	To remind citizens and registered taxpayers to pay their taxes, since 2008 a National Income Tax Day is celebrated.	Other government departments and Agencies Political leaders, Business organisations Civil society Popular national artists and sport icons	Internal		
Participation in Cultural Events of the Country	Burkina Faso	Organising national and international events and exhibitions designed to increase tax awareness and participation.		External	There is a sentiment of fear and suspicion among citizens towards tax services; they do not wish to have problems with the tax administration.	https://www.lefaso.net
"Tax and You" TV Show	Cote d'Ivoire	Educating taxpayers about their obligations and encouraging them to voluntarily comply via an informative TV show.	Media	External	TV is an effective vehicle for taxpayer education. It increases the perception among taxpayers of a moral obligation to pay taxes voluntarily.	
"Impôts, Késako" Website	France	Presenting taxes and explaining their evolution from the Ancient Regime to nowadays.		No		https://www.impots.gouv.fr/portail/www2/minisite/kezako/#page-top
"Strength Lies in Numbers" Festival	Guatemala	"Strength Lies in Numbers" is a festival organised every year by the SAT to promote positive tax culture and citizenship among different partner institutions and		No		

Title of the initiative	Country	Short summary	Partners	Evaluation	Lessons learnt	Useful links
		target groups. The first such festival was held in April 2008.				
TV Show "Citizens and Taxes"	Guinea	Bringing the administration closer to taxpayers with a TV show to better understand the public service character of the tax administration, the different types of taxes and the various means of payment that exist.		No	Need to continue this initiative and increase communication to favour more efficient taxpayer education.	
Madinati – an Educational Game on Taxpayer Compliance	Morocco	Transmitting the notions of collective goods and services, solidarity between citizens, and emphasising the necessity of paying collective expenses.	NA	No	The use of the game is relatively low; it needs to be accompanied by a wider communication campaign targeting children and teenagers.	
Sponsorship of Comedians/ Musicians	Nigeria	Targeting existing and potential taxpayers who are attracted to comedy and musical shows and events, with the aim of emphasising the need for them to be tax compliant.		No	Influencers (comedians/musicians) can make the message of taxation more palatable to the public. Their advocacy for tax compliance engenders a positive response from their audience and contributes to the widening of the tax net.	
Spleiselaget – A Website, Computer Game and Lecture to Discover Tax	Norway	Educating young people on the connections between tax, value creation, employment and undeclared work with a website, a computer game and lectures on the topics.	Labour unions Tax administration	External	Most participants are unaware of what tax money is used for, of the impact of undeclared work, and of what would happen to our society if there were more undeclared workers.	http://www.spleiselaget.no http://www.spleiselaget.no/byen http://www.spleiselaget.no/artikler/om-spleiselaget
Celebrating Taxpayers' Appreciation Day	Rwanda	Taxpayers' day has become a platform for dialogue, where RRA meets with the business community to talk about issues/challenges that may affect their businesses. It has also been a good framework for informing the community of what their taxes have achieved.	Private sector Federations at the national, provincial level and district level	External	It is necessary to streamline this initiative because it helps significantly in terms of improving voluntarily tax compliance. It has had an impact on increasing taxpayer confidence in the	https://www.youtube.com/watch?v=d9ycvsc7MI4 https://www.youtube.com/watch?v=DFHIH0cB6ek

Title of the initiative	Country	Short summary	Partners	Evaluation	Lessons learnt	Useful links
					tax administration	
National Information Days	Senegal	The 2016 edition of the taxpayer day was marked by an official ceremony organised outside Dakar – i.e., in Thiès, located 70 km from Dakar. At the local level, the tax authority's actions havehad considerable impact.	Ministry of education (in 2016)	No	The DGID must step up its communication activities. Dialogue and information for users are an excellent means of developing tax consent. Taxpayer services strengthen the trust relationship with users.	https://www.dakaractu.com/Journees-nationales-d-informations-et-de-sensibilisation-de-la-DGID-Sous-le-signe-de-la-promotion-du-consentement-a-l_a110542.html http://xalimasn.com/journee-dinformation-de-la-dgid-appel-au-civisme-fiscal/
TV Show "La Minute DGID"	Senegal	Providing simple, concise and accessible news and information about tax, land and cadastral themes via a TV show.	Media	No		
Weekly TV and Radio Shows	Togo	Informing, raising awareness among and educating taxpayers in the national territory with weekly TV and radio shows.	Government departments Unions	External	Need to keep the shows going to be in constant touch with the population, developing them to become more interactive.	https://www.otr.tg/index.php/fr/
Tax Week	Turkey	Celebrating Tax Week with country-wide campaigns to enhance tax awareness for children, taxpayers and all citizens.		No	New media instruments and effective communication techniques can improve compliance and increase the public image of the administration.	
The "Vergi Bilinci" (Tax Awareness) Training Programme for Children	Turkey	Raising tax awareness among the upcoming generation.	Government ministries	No	The administration is aware of the importance of educating children on tax awareness; therefore this initiative will be developed in terms of content and methods.	
Tax Facts	United Kingdom	Teaching tax through an educational programme for young people aged 8 to 19 years.	Educational Institutions Charitable Bodies	Internal	Young people appreciate how the programme is dispelling myths and giving an overview of what to expect when they start work. It is important to make the material fun and simple; it's	https://www.youtube.com/playlist?list=PL8EcnheDt1zjoRLU0l8WEKqgNzdR3w2xl https://www.tes.com/en-ie/teaching-resource/hmrc-junior-tax-facts-12106669

Title of the initiative	Country	Short summary	Partners	Evaluation	Lessons learnt	Useful links
					never too early to introduce people to the concept of tax.	
Annual Participation in the International Livestock Exposition and International Agro Industrial and Commercial Exhibition	Uruguay	Participating in international exhibitions with the aim of reaching not only the target audience but also citizens in general.		No	This initiative doesn't only reach children through educational activities, but also adults by presenting the work of the DGI from a different perspective.	www.dgi.gub.uy/educa
Tax Chat (radio)	Zambia	A weekly one-hour radio programme on Zambia's Radio Phoenix. This programme was initiated in March 2012 as a cost-effective alternative to television for reaching a wide target group.	Business agencies Government agencies Schools	This initiative was just one element in a broader evaluation.	It is important to keep records for accountability and to evaluate the engagement of each and every taxpayer, as well as to be consistent in maintaining frequently asked questions to determine where the knowledge gaps are.	

Source: OECD Survey on Taxpayer Education Initiatives, 2019.

Table A A.6. Tailoring messages to specific groups

Title of the initiative	Country	Short summary	Partners	Evaluation	Lessons learnt	Useful links
Use of Public Goods Messages in Reminder Letters on Personal Income Tax	Belgium	Sending letters to tax defaulters with information about the public goods and services provided by tax collection, to create an awareness of the importance of paying tax and to explain what tax money is used for.	Academic institutions	External	Behavioural insights influence tax compliance. Simplification and deterrence do better than tax morale in a Belgian Tax Context.	
Guidance for New Entrepreneurs	Finland	Ensuring that new entrepreneurs can fulfil their obligations easily and right from the start.		Internal	Guidance for new entrepreneurs must be produced and offered in	https://www.youtube.com/watch?v=JLGlsvagnvk

					various forms.	https://www.youtube.com/watch?v=_4xfk2OTTS4 http://verohallinto-en.mailpv.net/account
Annual Communications Programme for PAYE Taxpayers	Ireland	Writing letters to over 125 000 PAYE taxpayers annually to advise them of the range of tax credits and relief available, to remind them of the statutory four-year time limit in which to claim their entitlements, and to inform them of the need to advise revenue authorities of any additional income sources they may have.		External	Low-cost targeted education initiatives can have a relatively high impact on taxpayer behaviour in the targeted group.	https://www.revenue.ie/en/corporate/documents/research/taxpayer-entitlements.pdf https://www.revenue.ie/en/corporate/press-office/press-releases/2018/pr-011118-reminder-december-deadline.aspx https://www.revenue.ie/en/corporate/press-office/press-releases/2017/pr-231117-claim-tax-back-31-dec.aspx https://www.revenue.ie/en/corporate/press-office/press-releases/2016/pr-051216-entitlements-claim-deadline.aspx
Taxpayer Education Initiative Aimed at Foreign Workers and Corporate Income Taxpayers	Norway	Educating foreign personal and corporate income taxpayers through information dissemination and professional guidance in English in order to promote a culture of compliance.		Internal	It can be challenging to communicate important information to multicultural groups, especially where integration is limited; the language must be simplified and adapted.	www.skatteetaten.no/foreign
Support of Tax Compliance – Sending Informative E-mails to Citizens who are Starting Up an Activity	Portugal	Sending informative emails to young professionals to inform them of their tax obligations and to support tax compliance.	Academic institutions	No	It is important to simplify the language used in the communication with taxpayers. Being present among the taxpayers conveys proximity, transparency and reliability.	http://info.portaldasfinancas.gov.pt/pt/Cidadania/Paginas/default.aspx http://info.portaldasfinancas.gov.pt/pt/destaques/Paginas/at_contato_universidades.aspx
Online Support Sessions Through the NAFA's Facebook Page	Romania	Providing information to categories of taxpayers who cannot be reached through the classic channels of communication or who do not access the service channels provided by the tax agency.		No		
Information to Auditors and Diverse Industries	Sweden	Identifying facts that auditors and entrepreneurs in certain industries need, such as new legislation or information about areas where mistakes are often made.	Accounting industry	External		
Raising the Awareness of	Togo	Increasing the awareness of taxpayers and the public on taxpayer compliance by providing information to all	Government departments	Internal	The initiative should be repeated every year to	https://www.otr.tg/index.php/fr/

Taxpayers and the Public on Taxpayer Compliance		the population so that no citizen is left uninformed.	Media		achieve an increase in tax morale. It allows permanent contact between the tax administration and taxpayers.	

Source: OECD Survey on Taxpayer Education Initiatives.

Assisting taxpayers

Table A A.7. Assisting taxpayers in using tools

Title of the initiative	Country	Short summary	Partners	Evaluation	Lessons learnt	Useful links
Tutorial on How to Use the New Online Payment Application with a YouTube Video	Belgium	Explaining to taxpayers how to use the new online payment application with a YouTube video.		No	Mass media helps to spread these tutorials, but social media promotes them even further. It is important to make it as easy as possible to use the application in order to positively influence taxpayer behaviour.	https://youtube.com/watch?v=_iKP2M3dAm4
Digital Signature and Online Declarations	Colombia	A new digital signature supported by a digital certificate for documents and procedures carried out by individuals acting in their own name and/or representing or acting for another natural or legal person.		No		https://www.dian.gov.co/Prensa/Aprendelo-en-un-DIAN-X3/Paginas/Firma-Electronica.aspx
E-Filing	Egypt	Simplifying and modernising tax filing procedures with e-filing.		No		
Unified Tax Code	Egypt	A tax code to gather all existing laws.		No		
My Tax (New E-Service)	Finland	Offering communication and marketing initiatives for individual taxpayers.	Government agencies	Internal	It is important to plan the initiatives well and early on, and to make sure there is enough time and resources to execute them.	https://yle.fi/uutiset/osasto/news/finland_changing_income_tax_system_next_year/10440409 https://yle.fi/uutiset/osasto/news/revamped_online_system_puts_expanded_tax_data_at_users_fingertips/10500785

Title of the initiative	Country	Short summary	Partners	Evaluation	Lessons learnt	Useful links
Demonstration of the Taxpayer's Secure Web-Portal	Georgia	The GRS produced a demonstration version of its taxpayer's secure web-portal. The test version allows students (and other stakeholders) to familiarise themselves with the range of services provided by the GRS.		No		
Advertising Campaign on e-PIT	Hungary	Advertising electronic filling out of Personal Income Tax (PIT) returns, a topic involving more than five million taxpayers in Hungary. The tax administration has prepared pre-filled PIT returns for five years for every taxpayer on whom data are available. Thanks to this, the administrative burdens of private persons have been significantly reduced.	No	No	Every year when press reports are published, new ideas are needed because these innovative ideas – which do not lack humour – can sustain media interest.	www.nav.gov.hu www.facebook.com/navprofil
Educating Current and Potential Customers on Revenue's Online Portal "My Account"	Ireland	Improving the registration process for online services by providing instant retrieval of forgotten passwords and assisting customers in meeting their tax obligations and claiming their entitlements, at a time and place that is suitable to them.	Government departments	Internal	It is important to clearly communicate internally, among different areas, and also to consult with the end user of a development before making a final decision.	
PAYE Modernisation	Ireland	Modernising the PAYE system to switch from yearly reporting of payroll information to a real-time process.	Tax agencies Trade unions National associations	No	Communication and collaboration with both internal and external stakeholders are key to successful implementation.	
Pre-Filled Tax Return	Italy	Enhancing awareness and fostering the correct use of the pre-filled tax returns available online since 2015.	Government ministries Media	Internal	It is important to find the correct tone, language and media to communicate with different audiences. Moreover, it is fundamental to help taxpayers with e-services using new media (images, video, social).	https://infoprecompilata.agenziaentrate.gov.it/portale/ https://www.youtube.com/user/Entrateinvideo
E-Services Programme	Jamaica	Encouraging taxpayers to use the TAJ e-Services Platform to conduct business, in keeping with the TAJ's goals; encouraging the use of electronic platforms in its	Government agencies OECD	Internal and external	Taxpayers appreciate e-Services because of the benefits they gain from	https://www.jamaicatax.gov.jm/web/guest/how-to..

Title of the initiative	Country	Short summary	Partners	Evaluation	Lessons learnt	Useful links
		administration; and providing greater convenience to customers, while promoting the ease of doing business.			being able to access their accounts 24/7 and not having to go to tax offices. Providing access to computers and tax support is important, particularly for small businesses.	
Digitalisation of Property Tax Bills (e-PT Bill)	Singapore	Allowing property owners to obtain property tax information easily and proceed with payment seamlessly with digital bills.	Government departments	Internal	Need to apply the user experience design approach for future projects so that new services are built from the taxpayers' perspective.	https://www.straitstimes.com/business/invest/go-green-with-property-tax-notices https://www.straitstimes.com/business/property/property-tax-notices-to-go-electronic-though-opting-out-allowed-under-changes-up
INOA (Instantaneous Notice of Assessment)	Singapore	Enabling taxpayers to process their tax bills in real time and to experience a seamless online experience end-to-end thanks to instantaneous Notice of Assessment (iNOA).		Internal	It is prudent to have a contingency plan for potential risks that could hinder the stable implementation of the iNOA.	https://www.iras.gov.sg/irashome/News-and-Events/Newsroom/Media-Releases-and-Speeches/Media-Releases/2017/Tax-Season-2017---Maintained-Record-High-Overall-On-Time-Filing-Rate-of-96-/ https://www.straitstimes.com/singapore/iras-reminds-all-taxpayers-to-file-returns-from-march-1-to-april-18
Making Tax Digital	United Kingdom	Reducing errors in tax returns as well as the administrative burden on businesses by requiring them to keep their records digitally and submit their VAT returns through the UK's Making Tax Digital service.	Software developers Tax agents and accountants	No		https://www.gov.uk/government/collections/making-tax-digital-for-vat

Source: OECD Survey on Taxpayer Education Initiatives.

Table A A.8. Offering direct assistance

Title of the initiative	Country	Short summary	Partners	Evaluation	Lessons learnt	Useful links
Free Call Centre	Burundi	Communicating with taxpayers via telephone calls to provide information and advice, and answer enquiries related to tax.		No	For the initiative to be more successful, more local tax administrations need to be involved. Taxpayers also need to be convinced that their taxes contribute to the development of the country.	https://www.obr.bi/
Special Taxpayer Assistance Programme	Jamaica	Providing assistance to micro and small businesses to ensure that they fulfil their income tax filing obligation.	Business associations Government departments	No	If people are offered assistance they will comply. It is important to identify taxpayer education gaps.	http://tinyurl.com/yyhtfvaa http://tinyurl.com/y5cu2nub http://tinyurl.com/yxcpdys2
Tax Filing Support to Business	Korea	Supporting taxpayers' smooth tax filing (income tax, VAT) and application (ICL, EITC) procedures, and teaching them how to utilise already developed NTS system for taxpayers.		No	Although, the National Tax Service of Korea (NTS) has developed very advanced e-filing systems and infrastructure, many individual taxpayers and SMEs find it difficult to use the systems. For them, tax compliance is still something difficult and hard to understand.	
Support for Tax Compliance	Portugal	Supporting young professionals by providing them with information about tax obligations and the useful services available on the tax administration's website.	Academic institutions	No	There is a need to include tax education in school curricula. It is important to simplify the language used in communication with the taxpayer. Being present among taxpayers conveys more proximity, transparency and reliability.	http://info.portaldasfinancas.gov.pt/pt/Cidadania/Paginas/default.aspx http://info.portaldasfinancas.gov.pt/pt/destaques/Paginas/at_contato_universidades.aspx
"RRA IWACU" Awareness Campaign	Rwanda	Educating people that may not have the chance to attend the RRA education sessions with face-to-face sessions.	Private Businesses District Authorities	No	It is necessary to go out into the very rural areas to let everyone know about this initiative.	

Title of the initiative	Country	Short summary	Partners	Evaluation	Lessons learnt	Useful links
No-Filing Service (NFS)	Singapore	Under the NFS, taxpayers do not need to file a tax return if their employers have already transmitted their salaries to the Inland Revenue Authority of Singapore (IRAS) and they claim the same standard set of personal tax deductions each year.	Taxpayer representatives	Internal	Need to address taxpayers' concerns upfront and to provide them with reassurance.	IRAS Website https://www.iras.gov.sg/home Media Release – Filing tax less taxing now: https://www.straitstimes.com/business/invest/filing-tax-returns-less-taxing-now
Mobile Tax Units	South Africa	Mobile tax units utilise converted vehicles used as mobile offices as an innovative and cost-effective way to reach the neediest areas. They also cater to disadvantaged communities in South Africa.	National departments Municipalities Schools, via the Department of Education Hospitals, via the Department of Health The South African Medical Association Small business formations, via the Small Business Department Media organisations	Internal		
Information to Newly Started Businesses	Sweden	Helping newly started businesses understand what they need to do as entrepreneurs in terms of their responsibilities, rights and obligations.	Government agencies Organisations	Internal	The information helps new entrepreneurs start their businesses without making too many mistakes. Meeting them early in their entrepreneurship builds trust.	
The Tax Communication Centre	Turkey	Whenever taxpayers wish to reach any information related to tax, they can get it quickly via the Tax Communication Centre, first point of access for taxpayers seeking information from the Turkish Revenue Administration.		No	The training of the personnel as experts in their field provides more controlled and high-quality communication with	

Title of the initiative	Country	Short summary	Partners	Evaluation	Lessons learnt	Useful links
					taxpayers. The development and recruitment of services benefit from feedback given by taxpayers.	

Source: OECD Survey on Taxpayer Education Initiatives.

Cross-categories

Table A A.9. Núcleos de Apoyo Contable y Fiscal (NAF)

Title of the initiative	Country	Short summary	Partners	Evaluation	Lessons learnt	Useful links
Accounting and Tax Support in Universities	Argentina	Bringing tax administrations closer to citizens through the training of university students who assist low-income citizens in their basic tax obligations.	NGOs Government departments	No	Bringing the tax administration closer to universities removes practical difficulties when dealing with the management of the institutional page.	https://www.afip.gob.ar/educacionTributaria/
Accounting and Tax Support for Low-Income Taxpayers	Brazil	NAF are supported by tax administrations but run by universities through which students assist low-income taxpayers or small business owners.	Schools	No		https://www.gov.br/receitafederal/pt-br/assuntos/educacao-fiscal/educacao-fiscal/naf
Accounting and Tax Support in Universities	Chile	Working with institutions of higher education in tax and tax aspects, as well as linking students and institutions with the fiscal environment.	Academic Institutions	Internal	Students and the community are an important source of fiscal education: students are future professionals and taxpayers, and small businesses are supported in their formalisation.	
Accounting and Tax	Colombia	Strengthening public policies about taxpayer education, promoting tax culture, reducing inequalities, improving trust in institutions, facilitating the access to tax rights and	Government departments Academic	No	It is important to reach out to the communities that are the most in need, such as the	https://www.dian.gov.co/atencionciudadano/CulturaContribucion/Cultura-de-la-Contribucion/Paginas/Nucleos-de-Apoyo-

Support in Universities		services and fostering voluntary compliance.	institutions		lower-income population and those in zones mostly affected by the conflict (ZOMAC).	Contable-Fiscal.aspx
Accounting and Tax Support in Universities	Costa Rica	Informing professionals and students about the main tax duties with which they must comply when exercising their profession and explaining the social goal of taxation.	Academic institutions Government departments EUROsociAL	No	This is the most effective way to ensure that tax information is conveyed to students, with the advantage that the presenter is an official of the tax administration who is available for consultancies. There is a necessity to inform more widely of the means the Ministry puts at the disposal of tax education.	
Accounting and Tax Support in Universities	El Salvador	Empowering students who perform their social service, strengthening the social projection of universities, and joining alliances to support the Ministry of Finance in achieving its strategic objectives.	Academic institutions EUROsociAL	No	Knowledge about the topic contributes to better service.	
Accounting and Tax Support in Universities	Peru	Imparting to students of higher education basic knowledge about the tax system and customs of Peru, in order to complement their professional training and strengthen the tax and customs culture in the country.	Academic Institutions EUROsociQL	No	The NAF program encourages university students to become more involved in society by providing basic tax and customs guidelines and encourages them to become allies of the SUNAT.	https://cultura.sunat.gob.pe/nucleos-de-apoyo-contable-y-fiscal

Source: OECD Survey on Taxpayer Education Initiatives.

www.ingramcontent.com/pod-product-compliance
Ingram Content Group UK Ltd.
Pitfield, Milton Keynes, MK11 3LW, UK
UKHW051504290926
15471UKWH00008B/1409

9 789264 651579